THE CATHOLIC UNIVERSITY OF AMERICA

THE RÔLE OF THE VIRGIN MARY IN THE COVENTRY, YORK, CHESTER AND TOWNELEY CYCLES

A Dissertation

SUBMITTED TO THE FACULTY OF THE GRADUATE SCHOOL OF ARTS AND SCIENCES
OF THE CATHOLIC UNIVERSITY OF AMERICA IN PARTIAL FULFILLMENT
OF THE REQUIREMENTS FOR THE DEGREE OF DOCTOR OF PHILOSOPHY

BY

BROTHER CORNELIUS LUKE, F. S. C.

THE CATHOLIC UNIVERSITY OF AMERICA
WASHINGTON, D. C.
1933

ACKNOWLEDGMENT

This study arose out of a suggestion made by Associate Professor Francis J. Hemelt, of the Catholic University. For two years he patiently supervised its development and pointed out the chief directions it possibly could take. His unstinted and enlightening help was always mine to command. I hold myself very much indebted to him. I have likewise much reason for being grateful to two of my former students who unremittingly devoted all their energies to any task, great or small, I chose to give them in connection with the humbler but necessary aspects of getting ready the manuscript for printing. It is proper also to mention that I appreciate very much the courtesy and kindness so characteristic of the libraries of Congress and the Catholic University of America.

TABLE OF CONTENTS

INTRODUCTORY REMARK

The present study examines the rôle, and seeks to determine the status of the Virgin Mary as she appears in the four great cycles of the English medieval drama. It aims at establishing that her status in these cycles is thoroughly Christocentric,[1] and that she is dramatized consistently in the light of that status. If the view may not be as strikingly novel as not to have been sensed in its general pertinency by those who have intimately studied the cycle plays, still, a focussed and organized inspection of this aspect of the Marian rôle seems desirable, inasmuch as it threatens otherwise to be ignored.

Certain questions naturally spring up in connection with the inquiry that concerns this thesis, questions that I have answered in the supplementary remark, which follows the last chapter:

1. Does the apocryphal material frequently attached to the Virgin's rôle minimize the Christocentricity of her status in the plays?

2. What is specially characteristic of each cycle in its handling of the Marian rôle?

Moreover, to date, there has been no really serious inquiry into the rôle of the Virgin in the Middle English cyclic plays. Vriend [2] has offered a monograph which, though valuable, is much too discursive. Other scholars, such as Kretzmann [3] and Gayley,[4] allude to Mary *en passant,* but do not attempt a focussed study of her rôle. The *Planctus Mariae* has received considerable attention,

---

[1] I use this adjective, and the corresponding noun " Christocentricity," frequently and always to mean that the things I apply it to converge to Christ as a center.

[2] *The Blessed Virgin Mary in the Medieval Drama of England,* Purmerend, Holland, 1928.

[3] *The Liturgical Element in the Earliest Forms of the Medieval Drama,* Minneapolis, 1916.

[4] *Plays of Our Forefathers,* London, 1908.

particularly from Taylor [5] and Thien [6] in the English field.   The dramatic portion of the *Planctus,* however, perhaps by reason of its untraceable character, has not received concentrated attention. My study will include a discussion of the Virgin Mary in her rôle of Sorrowing Mother.

I have divided my treatment of the plays of each cycle into four chapters, treating each separate play, or parts of a play, in the time order of the episodes in which a harmonized Gospel narrative would present them.   The first deals with the Virgin in the Marian prophecies, which are quite interspersed throughout the cycles; the second has to do with her rôle in the plays whose stories deal with her life up to the birth of Christ; the third takes up her rôle in the plays extending to, but excluding the Passion plays; the fourth displays Mary's behavior in her rôle of Sorrowing Mother, and the dramatic treatment of her death, assumption, coronation, and apparition to Thomas.   In each of these chapters I have tried to disclose the Christocentric nature of the Virgin Mary's rôle, and the consistent recoil of the dramatists from any liberties that would allow her to be exploited to the detriment of her theological status as Mother of God and coredemptrix.   Following chapter four is a discussion given over to the two questions mentioned above.

To facilitate the following of the study, plays are listed in the table of contents under each chapter heading, according to the order in which they are studied.   I must point out, however, that those listed under Chapter I, with the exception of the *Prophets* of the Coventry cycle, do not receive separate discussion, for the reason that only fragments of each play are considered.   These fragments are grouped into a single discussion.   I have listed the plays throughout my study by designations that indicate the theme, rather than by the titles they are generally given.   This appears simpler, since on the one hand the traditional titles are often several and disconcerting, and on the other hand, the entitling of certain plays is arbitrary with editors.   The following are the texts I have used:

[5] "The English Planctus Mariae," in *Modern Philology,* IV (1907).
[6] *Über die Englischen Marienklagen,* Kiel Dissertation, 1907.

The Chester Plays, ed. by H. Deimling and Matthews, EETS. ES 62, 115 (1892, 1914) ;

Ludus Coventriae, ed. by K. Block, EETS. ES 120 (1917) ;

The Towneley Plays, ed. by G. England, EETS. ES 71 (1897) ;

York Plays, ed. by L. Smith, Oxford, 1885.

In recording the dates of Early English Text Society books I have used only the year that appears alongside of the work in the Early English Text Society tabulation.

CHAPTER I

This chapter, then, deals with the Marian element as alluded to in the various prophetic citations interspersed throughout the plays. The Coventry *Prophets,* being a complete unit, receives separate discussion. Though it does not dramatize any definite scriptural occurrence or anecdote, it naturally precedes the others, since of all the plays that lie within the scope of this study it is the only one whose theme comes within the chronology of the Old Testament. The play is, moreover, interesting to begin with, because its Marian element, emphatically present as it is, has nevertheless received but scant recognition by scholars who have undertaken to study the play. What they have said about it will be noted in its proper place within the compass of the next few pages.

We may call this prophet play in Coventry a transitional play from the Old Testament to the New; from the time of figures and signs to the time for fulfillment. The Old Testament sections of the Mysteries are really nothing more than modified prophet plays. To quote Greg:

> The Old Testament sections of the miracle cycles are, of course, not confined to the representations of prophets, but they are governed by what may be called the prophetic principle . . . They do not appear for their own sake, but for their relation to what follows: they are not themselves dramas, but dramatic prologues. The Fall is there as being implied by the Redemption, the Creation as the counterpart of Doomsday. The necessary data for their plot are given, otherwise it is for their prophetic significance that episodes are introduced. Some of the plays are actual prophet plays, many more concern the so-called types of Christ. . . . The extant English miracle cycles are not theatrical epics of universal history, but strictly dramas of the Redemption of man.[1]

As we come to the *Prophets* of Coventry, we find that the dramatic nexus between the Old and New Testaments is reached. Every succeeding play deals with New Testament themes, every previous play involves the Old Testament. The kings and prophets are

---

[1] *Bibliographical and Textual Problems of the English Miracle Cycles,* pp. 16-17.

dramatic remnants of the "things past," their utterances herald the "things to come." It is not at all surprising that the dramatist saw the fine appropriateness of making the Virgin the pivot-theme in this transition. The New Testament really begins with her, inasmuch as she was the providential instrument in bringing into the world the Maker of the New Testament.

MARY IN THE COVENTRY PROPHETS

The Coventry *Prophets* is unique among the English *Prophetae.* In the first place, the function of prophecy is given not only to prophets but also to kings. There are thirteen kings and thirteen prophets (Jesse excepted) and they speak alternately. Moreover, fifteen out of the total of twenty-seven prophecies allude, at least indirectly, to the Virgin Mary. Such peculiarities have given rise to some very interesting theories respecting the origin of the Coventry *Prophets,* which may well be mentioned here, since they have an important bearing on the present inquiry. The theories, of course, do not pivot upon a study of the Marian element. Their aim is to solve the origin of the play. Inasmuch, however, as my study, seeking as it does to learn the nature of the Marian element, will necessarily involve itself in an interpretation of the play as a whole, I shall state here the various viewpoints held by others who have given attention and study to the play.

Bonnell, whose conviction it is "that this single English play is directly influenced by—indeed, largely derived from—that pictorial representation of the genealogy of Christ which is known in art as *Tree of Jesse, Stirps Jesse,* or Radix Jesse," argues substantially thus:

The play ought to be called, not "The Prophets," but rather "The Tree of Jesse," or "The Rote of Jesse" (*Radix Jesse*). The title "The Prophets" does not occur in the manuscript, but was foisted upon the text by Halliwell, who mistook it for a simple evolution of the prophet play. The prologue itself suggests the probable title:

> Off þe gentyl *Jesse rote*
> þe sefnt pagent for sothe xal ben

Moreover, at the end of the play stands the rubric: *Explicit Jesse.*

Considering the play itself, we notice that Isaias, having uttered his familiar prophecy—*virgo concipiet et pariet filium*—is followed immediately by a speaker designated as *Radix Jesse* who, as it were taking the words out of the mouth of Isaias, utters that prophecy which, as we have seen, was the inspiration of artists:

> *Egredietur virga de radice Jesse*
> *Et flos de radice ejus ascendet,*

and continues, in his capacity of root of the genealogical tree, to speak about the branch and its flower that shall spring from him. David follows, and instead of choosing one of the many prophecies in his psalms, is content to announce himself the son of Jesse, the ancestor of Christ, and to echo the prophecy of Isaias. The alternating kings and prophets that follow indicate by their utterances in general that the genealogical tree is the central and dominant theme of the whole piece.

The thirteen prophets are most probably introduced to fill out a predetermined number. Although the *Processus Prophetarum* and the Limoges *Processus* have each thirteen prophets, the prophets of the Coventry play correspond with neither of these groups save in the case of Isaias, Jeremias, Daniel and Habacuc. Hence the play is evidently a dramatization of the iconographic *Tree of Jesse,* and as such can seem to have no ascertainable source save in art.[1a]

Kretzmann, however, cannot bring himself to accept Bonnell's theory, but argues convincingly and correctly it would seem, as follows:

> If there were no other prophet plays, if the influence of the Prophetae had not been so generally felt, if the prophets of the Coventry play . . . were altogether new and different from the other prophet plays, and, above all, if there were not so much evidence for direct liturgical basis also in this case, then one should not hesitate so much to accept Mr. Bonnell's conclusions. The fact that only four Augustinian prophets appear in the Coventry play is an argument which carries little weight, because . . . there are only two prophets in the Coventry list that have not appeared in a Latin liturgical play. . . . There can be no doubt that the *Radix Jesse* idea is liturgical. The Coventry author got his suggestion from the Matthew passage *lectiones,* with which the *Radix Jesse* was combined throughout the Church year.[2]

Hardin Craig believes that the Coventry *Prophets* " might be

---

[1a] " The Source in Art of the So-Called Prophets Play in the Hegge Collection," *PMLA.,* XXIX (1914), pp. 328 ff.

[2] *The Liturgical Element in the Earliest Forms of the Medieval Drama,* pp. 32-34.

described as a dramatic form of the medieval theme of the ' Root of Jesse.' They had . . . some special kind of prophet play known particularly as *visus,* or ' sights,' . . . and this Jesse, it is so called in the manuscript, with the accompanying virgin plays would be most appropriate." [3] In treating of this play Vriend concerns himself mainly with the non-Marian section, and constructs an argument (admittedly tentative), in which he would establish his opinion that

the pageant, from Solomon's prophecy onwards, is a recast of an older non-Marian prophet play, or perhaps of an apostle play, that is, of a Pentecost play, in which each of the twelve apostles enunciates an article of the creed.[4]

That statement is purely gratuitous. Shortly I shall show its untenability. So, evidently the Coventry *Prophets* is yet a fertile topic for investigation, worthy of many-sided study.

It may be well to note again that my study centers about the Marian element, and that whatever interpretation I think fit to place upon the play as a whole will be guided entirely by that study. An extraction of the Marian element, studied alongside the rest of the play, cannot but shed additional light, or at least incite others to further study from different angles.

To begin with, Bonnell, in clinging to his theme, namely, that the play is simply an attempt to dramatize the *Radix Jesse* iconograph, has quite apparently overlooked, or at the most, given little heed to the prominence of the Marian element. In the greater number of his citations from the kings and prophets, he has selected only those portions of their utterances that tend to confirm his theory regarding the theme of the play, seemingly ignoring the contexts. Among the lines which he has seen fit not to quote, the following allude to the Virgin:

David:

As God hym self hath mad promyssyon
Of Regall lyff xal come suche foyson
þat a clene mayde modyr xal be
Ageyns þe devellys fals illusyon
with regall power to make man fre.

---

[3] " Notes on the Home of Ludus Coventriae," in Swenson's *An Inquiry into the Composition and Structure of Ludus Coventriae,* p. 76.

[4] *The Blessed Virgin Mary in the Medieval Drama of England,* pp. 9-16.

Jeremias: [5]

> Affermynge pleynly be-forn þis Audyens
> That god of his high benyvolens
> of prest and kynge wyll take lynage
> And bye us alle ffrom oure offens
> in hevyn to haue his herytage.

Salamon:

> And þat wurthy temple for sothe made I
> which þat is fygure of þat mayde ȝynge
> þat xal be modyr of grett messy.

Abias:

> and sey also as in þis cas
> þat all oure myrth comyth of a mayd.

Asa:

> þat god wyll of a maydyn be born
> And vs to bryngyn to endles blys
> Ruly on rode be rent and torn.

Achas:

> þat falsly wurchepyd ydolatrye
> tyl Ysaie putt me in blame
> And seyd a mayd xulde bere messye.

Ezechias:

> My name is knowyn kyng Ezechyas
> þe xjte kyng of þis geneologye
> And say ffor sothe as in þis cas
> A mayde be mekenes xal brynge mercye.

Manasses:

> wyttnessynge here be trew testyficacion
> þat maydenys childe xal be prince of pes.

The Marian element is so prominent in these citations that we may well wonder why Bonnell so roundly overlooked it, especially in quoting. Certainly its very recurrence throughout the play might have elicited from him some admission as to its probable import, aside from the *Radix Jesse* iconograph. At any rate, Mary's rôle seems to have been pushed aside to make room for the *Radix Jesse* idea in his essay. Taking the play as a whole, we find that six prophets and eight kings allude to Mary, while the remaining seven prophets and five kings give voice solely to the

---

[5] This stanza contains no direct reference to the Virgin, but I insert it here on account of its line,

> of prest and kynge wyll take lynage

In the course of discussion I shall dwell on the immensely important bearing the line has upon the Marian element.

attributes of Christ and the incidents of His life on earth. Doubtless the Marian element here, which I shall treat of shortly, holds a
prominence that deserves particular study.

But I would first call attention to the fact that while the Marian
element stands out notably, it does not enter the focus. The prologue indeed tells us that " kings and prophets shall prophesy of
a queen-maid whom the fiends shall fear," but it also specifies her
Christocentricity: " Out of which maid doth spring our Healer,
as we read in prophecy. Her Son shall save us; be not dismayed
at His five wounds wide." And the play itself bears out this
Christocentric emphasis. The burden of every stanza is an utterance about Christ; and where allusion is made to Mary, it is always
set against the Christological background.

This Mariological prominence (fifteen out of the entire twenty-
seven stanzas allude, at least indirectly, to Mary) together with
the fact that the Mother of Christ is never mentioned apart from
Christ, led me to regard as inadequate the theory of Bonnell.
I have come to the conclusion that the Coventry *Prophets* is not,
as Bonnell suggests, " simply an attempt to dramatize the iconographic *Tree of Jesse,*" but that it is an attempt to show forth,
in dramatic form, the royal and sacerdotal lineage of Christ
through His Mother Mary.

There are several passages in the play itself that indicate its
theme:

Ysaias:

> Of Sacerdotale lynage þe trewth I ȝow tell
> Fflesch and blood to take god wyll be born
> Joye to man in erth and in hevyn Aungell
> At þe chyldys byrth joye xal make þat morn.

David:

> I am david of jesse rote
> the fresch kyng by naturall successyon
> *and of my blood xal sprynge oure bote*
> As god hym self hath mad promyssyon
> *Of Regall lyff xal come suche foyson*
> þat a clene mayde modyr xal be
> Ageyns þe devellys fals illusyon
> *with regall power to make man fre.*

Jeremias propheta:

> I am þe prophete Jeremye

And fullich a-corde in all sentence
with kyng dauid and with ysaie
Affermynge pleynly be-forn þis Audyens
That god of his high benyvolens
of prest and kynge wyll take lynage . . .
in hevyn to haue his herytage.

The scriptural basis of Christ's royal descent is clear enough. The evangelist, Matthew (I, 1-16), tracing the genealogy of Christ from Abraham, includes the royal line of Judean kings, beginning with David and ending with Jechonias.[6] This record is traced through the ancestry of St. Joseph, but St. Luke's genealogical tree of Christ (Luke III, 23-38), likewise traced through St. Joseph's ancestry, does not include the royal Judean line, although each evangelist has inserted David. However, the Davidic descent is established in either case, but how are we to account for the disparity? St. Joseph by nature was the son of Jacob. St. Matthew therefore calls Jacob the father of St. Joseph, and traces the genealogy accordingly. But the father of St. Joseph in the eyes of the law was Heli, through whom St. Luke accordingly traces the genealogy of Christ. The two histories are reconcilable, however, for the following reason, which is accepted by most exegetes. Jacob and Heli were brothers by the same mother, but not by the same father. Heli married and died without children. Jacob, according to law (Deut. XXV, 5), married his widow and begot Joseph. The evangelists, therefore, simply took each a different view of St. Joseph's parentage. Each pedigree converges at Zorobabel (Matt. I, 12; Luke III, 27), and each includes David (Matt. I, 6; Luke III, 31). Therefore each line illustrates the Davidic descent of Christ through the ancestry of St. Joseph. We

[6] There is a break in the genealogy, however, where it is written that Joram begot Ozias (Matt. i. 8). Three generations intervened before Ozias entered the line of Joram. The reasons alleged for this omission on the part of the evangelist are purely a matter of scriptural exegesis. For explanation, see *The Great Commentary of Cornelius à Lapide, St. Matthew's Gospel, Chapters I-IX*, tr. by T. Mossman, London, 1887, pp. 7-8; Maldonatus, *A Commentary on the Holy Gospels*, tr. by Daviem, London, 1888, pp. 10-12; MacEvilly, *An Exposition of the Gospels (Matthew and Mark)*, New York, 1888, pp. 5-6.

can readily perceive, though, with what greater clarity and vividness Matthew's account presents the Saviour's royal ancestral status, since that evangelist has included the line of kings, from David to Jechonias (Matt. I, 6-11).

Aside from genealogical records, the Gospel tells us more of Christ's Davidic descent. In St. Luke (I, 32, 69), we hear that the Child of Mary shall receive " the throne of David His father "; also, that in Christ, God " hath raised up an horn of salvation to us, in the house of David his servant." Again, in the Epistles, St. Paul tells us that Christ " was made . . . of the seed of David, according to the flesh " (Rom. I, 3).

The question now arises (and an all-important question it is in this discussion), Was Mary also of Davidic descent? That she was, is clear from the statements in St. Luke and St. Paul, cited immediately above. Surely if she were not of Davidic descent, her Son, conceived without the intervention of man, could not be said to be " of the seed of David." Many commentators, seeking more securely to establish the Virgin's Davidic descent, interpret St. Luke's genealogy as referring to Mary rather than to Joseph.[7] Medieval writings, together with the plays themselves, testify that Mary's Davidic lineage was a medieval tradition, at least in England. Thus, in the medieval version of the life of St. Anne we are told she is sprung " of the stok of Dauid." [8] And inferentially we learn it from the *Cursor Mundi,* which pronounces Joachim, father of Mary, to be sprung of Jesse's Root, descended from ' gentle King David.' [9] The *Golden Legend* offers a painstaking explanation of how Mary was the recipient of the blood royal and the sacerdotal heritage.[10] The explanation here is identical with that given by St. Augustine.[11]

---

[7] A detailed discussion is given by A. J. Maas, " The Blessed Virgin Mary," in *Catholic Encyclopedia,* XV (1913), 464. I have not found evidence anywhere that St. Luke's table was ever interpreted thus in the Middle Ages.

[8] *The Middle English Stanzaic Version of the Life of St. Anne,* ed. R. E. Parker, London, 1928. EETS. OS., 174, p. 98.

[9] *Cursor Mundi,* ed. Morris, London, EETS., in seven volumes.

[10] *La Légende Dorée,* tr. by Roze, Paris, 1902, III, 11-12.

[11] See Livius, *The Blessed Virgin in the Fathers of the First Six Centuries,* London, New York, 1893, p. 133.

Then there is Christ's claim to the sacerdotal status, as sounded in the play by *Ysaias,*

> Of Sacerdotale lynage þe trewth I ȝow tell

and *Jeremias,*

> Of prest and kynge wyll take lynage.

This character of Priest, in Christ, derives from Mary, into whom the sacerdotal descent flowed from her mother, Anne. That St. Anne is the traditional mother of the Virgin need not be discussed in detail. The matter is not mentioned in Scripture, but derives, it would seem, from the apocryphal *Gospel of James,* the *Nativity of Mary,* and the *Pseudo-Matthew Gospel.*[12] At any rate, the Church has sanctioned the tradition from early times, and the St. Anne cult has long been one of the most widespread in Christendom.[13] Now the idea of Christ's sacerdotal descent is derived ultimately from the tradition that Anne herself was a daughter of Aaron. This is not recorded in Scripture, nor even, as far as I have been able to determine, in any of the apocryphal writings. However, there can be no doubt that the idea was traditional. St. Augustine explains it thus:

> The sacerdotal line differed from the royal line, which had its origin in one of David's sons, who, according to the custom, married a wife from the sacerdotal line. Hence Mary belonged to both tribes and had her descent in the royal and sacerdotal line.[14]

The *Golden Legend* adopts this explanation.[15] In the *Life of St. Anne,* the author, comparing Anne to Juda and Levi, says:

> Among whom Iudas and Leui do shyne
> Before all other there most myghtyly;
> Of whom the kyngdom and presthode by lyne
> Of the same pepyll ys gon out truly.
> The corner stone Cryst hath bound hem surely
> Togedyr as two stone walles most sure
> In the blyssyd Anne, modyr clene and pure.[16]

---

[12] See M. James, *The Apocryphal New Testament,* Oxford, 1924.
[13] See Holweck, " St. Anne," in *Catholic Encyclopedia* I (1913), 538 ff.
[14] See Livius, *op. cit.,* p. 133.
[15] *Op. cit.,* pp. 11-12.
[16] *Op. cit.,* p. 97. An account of Christ as mystical High Priest is given by St. Paul, Heb. v. viii. ix. x.

I have found the tradition to exist among a number of Ethiopian legends of the Blessed Virgin from fifteenth century manuscripts. The editor and translator of this corpus of legends, Wallis Budge, remarks in his introduction that the legends bear indication of having been derived from western European tradition regarding the Virgin. The text reads:

> For this reason I preach and I tell the story of the birth of our Lady Mary from the loins of Joachim, the staff of the kingdom, and from the womb of Hanna, the staff of the priesthood. Come then, O ye prophets of the Good God, and be ye my helpers that I may declare the sweetness of the glory of your daughter, the mother of light.[17]

At any rate, we note that the sacerdotal line and the royal Davidic line were looked upon to converge in Mary, who, by giving birth to Christ, imparted both characters to Him. This is the foundation of the statements found in the *Coventry Prophets Play,* the *Golden Legend* and the *Life of St. Anne,* regarding the dual heritage of Christ.

But this point leads us into an analysis of the play itself; an analysis which, I feel, establishes definitely that the piece is not, as Bonnell wrote, simply an attempt to dramatize the iconographic *Tree of Jesse,* nor, as Vriend postulates, a development or interpolation of older plays, but rather that it is a separate, complete and unaltered dramatization of the royal and sacerdotal genealogical status of Christ through His Mother Mary.

The first clue to the theme of the play occurs at the very beginning, in that line of Isaias:

> Of Sacerdotale lynage þe trewth I ȝow tell . . .

Inasmuch as anything concerning the coming of Christ can be introduced by nothing more appropriate than Isaias' remarkable utterance: *Ecce Virgo concipiet, et pariet Filium,* we are not surprised to hear this prophecy above all others falling from the lips of the greatest prophet of Christ's advent. David, the first king to appear, (I am omitting *Radix Jesse* for the present but shall consider his rôle shortly) forcefully proclaims the regal rights and powers of the Child that is to spring from his blood through

[17] Budge, *Legends of Our Lady the Perpetual Virgin and Her Mother Hanna,* Boston, 1922, p. 2.

the Virgin Mary; and Jeremias, the very next prophet, combines
the dual idea of priesthood and kingship:

> And fullich a-corde in all sentence
> with kyng dauid and with ysaie . . .
> That god of his high benyvolens
> *of prest and kynge wyll take lynage*

In other words, Isaias has announced the first part of the motif,
King David the second, and Jeremias has set forth the dual idea
as one. Since both Isaias and King David have also announced
the medium by which Christ's royal and sacerdotal lineage is
transmitted, there is no need for Jeremias to reiterate the mention
of Mary. His rôle consists in completing the prologue of the
play, as it were, by stating the theme in its whole form. From
here on, kings and prophets alternate, all testifying to Christ,
some to Christ through Mary. This continuity of alternating
king and prophet denotes the symbolical parentage of Christ, represented from the beginning by Isaias and David, the one announcing the priesthood, the other the royalty of Christ. Herein
is the explanation of that rather strange assortment of prophets.
Bonnell has pointed out that some of them are given utterances
not historically theirs, while others merely echo the prophecy of
Isaias. Right here is where the playwright's intention manifests
itself. His aim cannot have been other than to produce a balance
with the thirteen kings, which balance cannot be otherwise explained
than as a means of representing the dual ancestry. That is really
why not all the prophets utter things canonically ascribed to them.
The author was more concerned with visually establishing this
dual lineage than with putting into the mouth of every prophet
the proper lines. Moreover, since this ancestry was to converge
in Christ's Mother, Mary is frequently alluded to. This undoubtedly accounts for the frequent echoing of the prophecy of Isaias.
Prophets, introduced for a symbolical purpose only, and having
but little relevant to say of their own, could not do better than
fall back upon the initial prophecy of the play.

There is one other thing important to note regarding the
prophets in this play. They are all prophets of the kingdom of
Juda. Other prophets equally popular might have been introduced, such as Elias and Eliseus, or even Balaam, Malachias,

Jacob and Moses, all of whom uttered prophecies very pertinent to Christ's coming; still, the author selected only Judean prophets. This selection seems to argue conclusively against the possibility of the Coventry *Prophets* being a development or an interpolation of other prophet or Marian plays, since Judean prophets indicate a compactness that could not very well characterize a developed or interpolated play. The Judean prophets add unity to a play that purposes in part to establish the royalty of Christ, which royalty resided, of course, only in the tribe of Juda. I might indicate here an instance in the *Life of St. Anne* [18] which fits in nicely with the idea in hand. When Mary is proposed by the High Priest for marriage, the twelve tribes of Israel cast lots for her hand and she falls to Juda. Here too I might point out that in this Coventry play the words of both kings and prophets, regarding Our Lord's life on earth, cannot very well be construed into the remnants of a creed play, since, as I have already observed, the author's concern was mainly to represent Christ's ancestry by these characters; hence, in most cases, the characters having nothing of themselves in particular to utter, their sayings had to be selected at random. And a chronological account of Christ's life would appear most appropriate under the circumstances, just as an echoing of Isaias was the most appropriate dictum to put into the mouths of those prophets who likewise had nothing of their own to say. Lastly, the fact that the prophets are by no means chronologically ordered signifies that they are not there for any inherent purpose, but only to fit into the symbolical balancing of Christ's royal-sacerdotal descent. Isaias might be considered present through express design, since he is the supreme prophet of Christ's advent, and expressed the supreme prophecy of Mary, her maternity and her virginity. He appears in all the cycles. Jeremias, also, is appropriate here, since he himself was a high priest, and thus might aptly symbolize Christ, the supreme High Priest. Ezechiel was also of the priestly race.

So much for the prophets. Turning now to a detailed study of the kings in this play, we are confronted with a difficult question. Just why there are thirteen selected, with Josias and

[18] *Op. cit.*, p. 13.

Jechonias omitted, is a problem hazardous to pronounce absolutely upon. Bonnell has helped greatly by pointing out that both the *Pseudo-Augustinian Sermon* and the Limoge *Processus* have each thirteen prophets.[19] It seems to me that the idea was not original with the author of the Coventry *Prophets,* but rather that he derived his scheme from some precedent. And the most probable precedent was the recurrence of the number in the two above mentioned pieces. Bonnell's objection to this theory on the ground that between our play and the other two pieces there is community of only four prophets—Isaias, Jeremias, Daniel and Habacuc—is easily answered if we remember that of the entire number of prophets mentioned in the *Sermon* and in the *Processus* of Limoge, only four were Judeans, and these four happen precisely to be Isaias, Jeremias, Daniel and Habacuc. It would seem natural, after all, for a medieval playwright to keep on the alert for suggestive material. Herein, at least, it would appear that our author adopted the number of prophets contained in the *Sermon* and *Processus,* together with as many of the actual prophets as would accommodate his theme. Granted this conjecture as true, we consequently have no difficulty in perceiving why a corresponding number of kings should be selected, even at the expense of omitting the last two of the line. At any rate, though I by no means consider the question solved, I do hold that, as far as research has thus far availed, my theory is as tenable as can be expected. The choice seems actually to lie between accepting this theory or admitting despairingly of a high eccentricity on the part of the playwright.

There is another peculiar feature to be observed regarding the kings. Each is made to speak. Vriend points out that this particular feature cannot have derived itself from art, since nowhere, among the extant *Radix Jesse* iconographs, are kings, besides prophets, provided with scrolls. Vriend,[20] after painstaking research, has nowhere been able to discover an instance of such an iconograph. At most, the only information given of the kings is their names. But when we consider that the kings, alternating as they do, with the prophets, are there to testify to Christ's royal descent, we are not at all surprised to hear them alluding to the

---

[19] *Op. cit.,* p. 336.   [20] *Op. cit.,* p. 16.

King of Kings and to His Mother, in whom both the sacerdotal and the royal bloods were confluent. In other words, the speeches of the kings are determined by the architectonics of the play, just as were the uncanonical speeches of the prophets.

The kings, then, are present solely to testify to Christ's royal descent. Their speech concerns itself either directly with Christ, with some incident in His life, or indirectly with Him through Mary, alluding to her via the prophecy of Isaias. They sometimes include Mary, as do the prophets, because it is she who is to impart the royal character to Christ, since in her the royal and sacerdotal lineage flow as one stream. They alternate with the prophets to represent symbolically the dual ancestry of Christ. Moreover, the fact that of the kings themselves not more than three are recorded as having remained faithful to the Lord (Josaphat, Joatham, Ezechias) indicates that they are there, not for inherent qualities, but solely to testify to and establish Christ as legal heir to King David, through Mary.

I wish now to consider the *Radix Jesse* theme, made so much of by Bonnell. It is undeniable that the theme is actually present in the piece, but it is equally undeniable that it by no means forms the motif, as Bonnell contended. It is present, but merely as a *utility* for imparting a thread of continuity to the play. We can easily understand how the idea of the royal descent of Christ must inevitably have linked itself up with the *Radix Jesse* idea, for, aside from the fact that Jesse, in the genealogies recorded by both Luke and Matthew, is father of David, and also apart from the fact that the prophecy of Isaias—*Egredietur virga de radice Jesse* . . . —added higher and more mystical meaning to that fatherhood, thereby inseparably linking Christ's regal descent with His more ultimate descent from Jesse, we also find abundance of testimony to the wide vogue of the *Radix Jesse* theme in the liturgy.[21] Hence we cannot conceive of the playwright's omitting a feature which so intimately links itself up with the theme of Christ's royal descent. Besides, if the motif of the play were really the *Radix Jesse* theme, we should expect a deeper emphasis upon it. As it is, only seven out of the total of thirteen kings announce themselves

[21] See Kretzmann, *op. cit.*, pp. 31-32.

as sprung of Jesse's root, and yet we should expect even more, considering that the theme is quite inseparable from the idea of Christ's royal lineage.   And more than this: If the play were really a dramatization of the *Radix Jesse* iconograph, might we not expect the prophets to be rather emphatic upon the theme?   As it is, Daniel's prophecy might appear to bear some such emphasis:

> I prophete Danyel am well apayed
> in fygure of þis I saw a tre
> all þe fendys of hell xall ben affrayd
> whan maydenys ffrute þer on þei se.

Bonnell remarks that this prophecy "seems to be an incorrect allusion to *Daniel* IV, 10 et seq., wherein we read of Nabuchodonosor's vision of a great tree reaching to heaven." [22]   He then opines that the author of the play introduced this vision in order to have a prophecy appropriate to the tree of Jesse.   But the conclusion does not *de facto* follow.   I rather feel that Daniel's distorted interpretation of that vision of Nabuchodonosor should excite no surprise, since, as Bonnell himself points out, the playwright has not been at all scrupulous regarding the clarity and accuracy of some of the prophecies.   Now, I should not at all wonder if Daniel also were made to twist his prophecy in such fashion in order to obtain a phraseological similarity with a certain line in the Prologue:

> *Prologue:*   All ffendys of here xal be Affrayde
>
> *Danyel:*   all þe fendys of hell xall ben affrayd

At least, there is the suggestion of accommodation.   Aggeus, however, is not necessarily referring to the *Jesse* theme, as Bonnell believes, when, replying to Joachim Rex, who has stated that God shall come of his "kynrede," he says:

> With 3ow I do holde þat am prophete Aggee
> Com of þe same hygh and holy stok
> god of oure kynrede in dede born wyl be
> Ffrom þe wulf to saue al shepe of his flok.

Here, it seems to me, the prophet is merely alluding to the royal line of Christ, not necessarily to the *Jesse* idea.   Moreover, Bonnell

[22] *Op. cit.,* p. 334.

is not justified in saying that in these lines, " prophecy is subordinated to the claim of kinship in the same high and holy stock." [23] Line two would seem much more logically and correctly interpreted as referring to line three rather than to line one. Aggeus, though Judean, decidedly was not of the royal line. Else we should have to admit an idiosyncracy of the author highly inconsistent with the rest of his plays.

One word more regarding the *Radix Jesse* theme. Those kings who claim descent from Jesse are evidently much more concerned with affirming their kingship. Christ of course receives the whole and ultimate emphasis, but their kingship is second, and the *Jesse rote* theme last in emphasis. Allusions to *Jesse* by the kings seems made only out of deference, or reverence. And seven—barely more than half, are that reverential. All, however, are careful to assert their kingship.

The *Radix Jesse* idea, then, is merely utilized in the play, incorporated into it as an unavoidable theme. But it is decidedly not the motif of the play, as Bonnell has thought it to be. Although all that has gone before illustrates fully that it is through Mary the dual lineage of Christ is transmitted, a word of summary regarding her rôle will not be amiss.

First of all, Mary's rôle in the play is purely Christocentric. She is portrayed entirely in the light of her motherhood of Christ. Then too, the presence of the theme of Mary's parentage in Joachim and Anne indicates the influence of the elaborate tradition and devotion that surrounded that theme, especially in medieval times. Mary, moreover, though not (I repeat it) the primary personage of the play, is really a pivotal point, so to speak, since she is the medium between Christ and the dual heritage that descended to Him. Hence the prominence accorded her by both king and prophet.

[23] *Ibid.*, p. 335.

OTHER MARIOLOGICAL PROPHETIC THEMES IN THE CYCLES

I have just given special attention to the Coventry *Prophets* because as I said at the outset, and later demonstrated, although the Marian element is there recognized well enough, its relation to the play proper is misunderstood. I have now to consider additional instances of prophecy involving the Mother of God, appearing in the York, Chester and Towneley cycles. It would be a tempting, but too digressive a matter here to rehearse the various arguments brought forth by scholars in an effort to establish whether or no the prophecies in the mystery plays are dependent on the *Pseudo-Augustinian Sermon*.[24] A reference is all that this study may admit of.[25] The status of Mary as she is involved in the prophecies must alone occupy us here.

We note first of all that nowhere among these prophecies is the Marian element dissociated from the idea of Christ. The very background of each utterance is Christ; and it is only as Mother of Christ that Mary is alluded to. The various contexts in the plays themselves will illustrate this point. In Chester, for example, *Expositor* explains the *Virgo concipiet* prophecy of Isaias thus:

> Lordinges, these wordes are so veray
> that exposition, in good faye,
> none needes, but you know may
> this word Emanuell.
>
> Emanuell is as much to saye
> as 'God with us night and day,'
> therfore that name for ever and aye
> to his sonne cordes wondrous well.

---

[24] This is a sermon probably written in the sixth century, but ascribed throughout the Middle Ages to St. Augustine. It is contained in Migne's *P. L.*, LII, 1125-1127. For a discussion on its dramatic import, see Studer, ed., *Le Mystère d'Adam*, Manchester, 1918, Introd., pp. xii ff.

[25] Sepet, *Les Prophètes du Christ*, Paris, 1878.
  Louis Petit de Julleville, *Les Mystères*, Paris, 1880, II; *Les Comédiens en France au moyen âge*, Paris, 1885.
  E. K. Chambers, *The Medieval Stage*, Oxford, 1903, II.
  O. Cargill, *Drama and Liturgy*, New York, 1930.
  G. Coffman, *Speculum*, VI (1931), No. 4, pp. 610-617.
  Kretzmann, *op. cit.*
  P. Studer, *loc. cit.*

There are other instances where the topic almost immediately shifts from the Virgin to Christ. The first prophecy of Isaias in York immediately switches into a discussion upon the royalty of Christ. Likewise Balaam's mention of Mary in the York Shepherd play seems more or less incidental to the prime topic, the new born Babe. And in the other contexts to these prophecies, in which Mary receives a more extended discussion, even there we notice the same manifest contribution to the Christocentric theme.

Worthy again of note is the recurrent allusion to Mary as Virgin. We have seen this same refrain in the Marian prophecies of the Coventry *Prophets.* That it was quite impossible to refer to Mary as Mother of God without expressing that prerogative in terms of her virginity is evident to Catholic and non-Catholic alike.[26]

Several inaccuracies in the prophecies enable us to see conclusively that when the dramatists wrench a scriptural utterance to make it embody a mention of the Virgin, they are doing so only to juxtapose Mary to her Son, and to emphasize thus the theme of Mother and Son. This tendency, so manifest up and down the cycles wherever Mary is concerned—even, as I shall show, in such plays as *Mary in the Temple,* and *The Conception of Mary*—is a clear echo of the medieval Virgin cult. It was really a movement of humanization, out of which eventuated the *Planctus Mariae* devotion—a topic that is to concern us in the fourth chapter of this work. It is usual to consider St. Bernard the most responsible factor in this humanization. We must remember that in the writings of the Fathers,

the humanity of Our Lord seldom appears except as the instrument of the Word. In Christ it is chiefly the Divinity that stands out, because it is the Divinity which was denied by the Christological heresies and by that other heresy, Pelagianism, which by its denial of original sin and the necessity of grace, denied also the necessity for redemption and a Redeemer; or, if Christ is contemplated in His two natures, God and Man, it is not as the Crucified, our Brother in affliction and in love, but the Conqueror, the King of Glory; *regnavit a ligno Deus.*[27]

St. Bernard, however, with contemporary mystics, humanized the

---

[26] See also Pourrat, *Christian Spirituality,* II, 51-60.

[27] Vernet, *Medieval Spirituality,* London, 1930, pp. 91-92.

love of men for Christ. He himself is moved to devotion by every detail of Christ's life. The following is a typical prayer of his:

I salute thee, my beloved Jesus! I desire always to cling to Thy Cross, and Thou knowest why. Come to my aid. Look down upon me from Thy Cross, O Beloved of my soul; draw me all to Thyself, only say to me: "I will heal thee and I will forgive thee all." Inflamed with Thy love and overwhelmed with shame, I embrace Thee and I cling to Thee . . .[28]

Pourrat has nicely expressed the whole idea when he says:

Ever since the twelfth century the writings of St. Bernard turned hearts towards the mysteries of the earthly life of Jesus, particularly toward those of His birth and passion. . . . At the beginning of the fourteenth century, under the influence of St. Francis of Assisi and the *Mystery Plays*, the faithful were moved to tender feeling at the sight of the Child Jesus in His crib, and especially by Christ dying on the Cross.[29]

I have introduced this data to show that the constant juxtaposition of Mother and Child was most probably influenced by the spread of the humanization that was promoted by St. Bernard. It seems obvious to me that the part assigned to Mary in this relation is purely Christocentric, for it is purely orthodox. Although worship is tendered the Virgin, it is apparent that this worship befalls her only in virtue of her divine maternity. The medieval devotion to Mary was Christocentric, just as was the devotion of the Fathers to Mary; but each was modified by the philosophic world-view of early and later Christianity. Here in these plays we perceive an evident devotion to Mary, but because it was staged we cannot thereby conclude that it degenerated into a sort of dramatic exploitation. Nor because it is humanized can we say that it is any the less Christocentric, since from the eleventh century onward this humanization was much the vogue, both in England and on the Continent,[30] and suffered no loss of orthodoxy, either in its humanizing the cult of Christ or that of His mother. This juxtaposition of Mother and Child, as apparent in the prophecies and in all the

[28] *Ibid.*, p. 90.

[29] *Christian Spirituality*, II, 319. Pourrat also provides a bibliography of Medieval mystical writings showing the development of this movement. *Ibid.*, p. 320.

[30] Cf. W. Ward, "The Origins of English Drama," in *The Cambridge History of English Literature*, V (1910), 47.

cycles, clearly testifies to the unchanged Christocentricity of Mary's rôle.

A notable misconstruction, or misinterpretation of prophecy, occurs in the utterance of Isaias in the Towneley Shepherd Play, I. One of the shepherds seems to be confusing *Egredietur virga de radice Jesse* (Isa. XI, 1) with *Ecce virgo concipiet et pariet filium* (Isa. VII, 14), for he takes *virga* for something like a variant reading of *virgo*:

> Also Isay says our faders vs told
> That a vyrgyn shuld pas of Jesse, that wold
> Bryng furth, by grace a floure so bold;
> That vyrgyn now has these wordys vphold
> As ye se;
> Trust it now we may,
> he is borne this day,
> Exiet virga
> De radice jesse.

Doubtless this confusion arose from an unlettered acquaintance with the Sarum response used in the liturgy of the Mary festivals:

> *stirps Jesse virgam produxit, virgaque florem,*
> *Virgo Dei Genetrix est, flos filius ejus.*[31]

This almost juxtaposition of *virgo* and *virga* must have suggested some mysterious connection to the medieval mind, which was always on the lookout for Old Testament types prefiguring New Testament personages. Vriend [32] cites a medieval exegete (Petrus Comestor) who attempted to establish this very connection.[33] St. Thomas, too, has an elaborate sermon on the subject.[34]

The Towneley prophecy of Moses also involves a prefiguration. The text has it thus:

Tertius pastor:

> Of hym spake Ieromy and moyses also,
> Where he sagh hym by a bushe burnand, lo!
> when he cam to aspy if it were so,
> Vnburnyd was it truly at commyng thereto,
> A wonder.

---

[31] Cf. Kretzmann, p. 31.
[32] *Op. cit.*, p. 19.
[33] Migne, 198, 1723.
[34] Opera 15, 211 (Parmae, 1864).

Primus pastor:

> That was for to se
> hir holy vyrgynyte,
> That she vnfylyd shuld be,
> Thus can I ponder,
> And shuld haue a chyld sich was never sene.

A parallel is seen in Chester,[35] when the newly risen Christ, speaking to the disciples of Emmaus, says:

> And first at Moses to beginne,
> what he sayeth I shall you minne,
> that God was a Greave within,
> that burned aye as hym thought.

> The Greave payred nothing therby:
> what was that but mayd Mary,
> that bare Iesu Sinlesly,
> that man hath now forbought?

Hemingway [36] has cited a similarity in lines from Chaucer. The same prefigurement exists in the *Rubum quem viderat Moyses* antiphon in the *Little Office of the Blessed Virgin.*

Further " adaptations " of the various dramatists are seen in:

(a) Balaam's Prophecy. In York [37] and Coventry [38] his prophecy of a star rising is associated with the motherhood of the Virgin Mary. The extension goes even farther in the Magi story in the *Pageant of the Shearmen and Taylors,*[39] for here the phenomenon of the rising star is associated with Isaias rather than with Balaam.

(b) Jeremias' prophecy in Chester.[40] The dramatist makes the " virgin " of Jeremias (XIV, 17) refer to Mary as Sorrowing Mother. All these prophetic " adaptations " to the Marian theme likewise associate her with Christ, in fact, are doubtless expressly meant to portray her Christocentric status. No amount of juggling

---

[35] MS No. 19.

[36] *Op. cit.*, p. 282. Chaucer, however, and likewise our playwrights, were drawing from the Christian tradition of the immaculate purity of the Mother of God. The prefiguration had more than an imaginative basis.

[37] MS No. 15.

[38] MS No. 18.

[39] Craig, *Two Coventry Plays*, EETS. ES. (1902), 87.

[40] MS No. 5.

20768

between the originals and their interpretation alters that status. They point rather to the purposeful design of the dramatists to emphasize her maternal relations with the Saviour. Her virginity is stressed in the case of Moses' prophecy similarly to underline this concomitant prerogative with her divine maternity. The context of that instance also shows a Christocentricity rather than a concentration upon Mary as an individual.

Amos [41] recalls to us the meaning of Mary's entering into the state of marriage, namely to conceal Christ's divinity from the devil.[42] The York *Harrowing of Hell* echoes the theme when Christ addresses Satan:

> Mi godhede here I hidde
> In Marie modir myne,
> For it schulde no3t be kidde,
> To þe nor to none of thyne.

In these prophecies the Virgin is represented fundamentally as Mother of God. This Christocentricity is apparent in whatever direction we look among the scattered prophecies. It is equally indisputable, I think, that the humanization of the Christ and Mary cult has strongly influenced the juxtaposition of Mother and Child so manifest in these prophecies. But as this humanization, as far as Mary was concerned, retained and even emphasized her Christological status, there can be no reason for supposing that her status should be dropped in the play, or that it should be tainted with the slightest dramatic exploitation, even in mere allusion to her. Then too, the prophetic " adaptations," or changes, which I have pointed out, do not compromise her Christocentric character, but appear to be designedly used to enhance that character. I have also indicated that the emphasis laid upon Mary's virginity refers solely to her prerogative of Mother of God. Here, as in other instances, the Virgin's rôle tends purely to emphasize the Christ.

---

[41] Y. MS No. 12.
[42] See also Hemingway, *op. cit.*, p. 215, and *Cursor Mundi*, II, 10783 ff.

CHAPTER II

The following group of plays comprises a dramatization mostly
of apocryphal material. All, with the exception of the *Salutation
and Conception, Joseph's Return,* and the *Visit to Elizabeth* have no
scriptural basis. *Joseph's Return* receives in general a good deal
of embroidery over the brief and delicate account of the Gospel.
My discussions of the various plays will show that there is a guid-
ing restraint in the handling of the Virgin's rôle in the midst of
abundant apocryphal elements.

We turn first to those plays that mark the early life of the Virgin.
In the Coventry cycle the five plays immediately following the
Prophets (*Joseph's Return* excepted) constitute what is generally
regarded as the Virgin Group. Interesting discussion has arisen
over this group of plays. Miss Block,[1] the latest editor of the cycle,
believes that the Virgin Group is a composite of two older cycles.
Miss Swenson[2] maintains that it consists of an interpolation of
new plays into an old group which has been modified for the
purpose. Chambers,[3] and Hardin Craig[4] after him, have both been
led by the prominence of St. Anne in several of the plays to assign
their staging to some St. Anne festivals, while in his preface to
the stanzaic versions of the *Life of St. Anne,* Parker[5] has taken
pains to show that the plays, with the exception of the *Visit to
Elizabeth,* are built upon the *Life of St. Anne,* and that they were
performed most probably by a St. Anne's guild. But we shall
prescind from the questions involved in the origin of this set of
plays, and limit ourselves to an inspection of their Marian element.
Whatever else may be said about it, one thing stands out in the
Virgin Group: its deep ecclesiastical coloring. And whether or
not a cleric or a religious composed the group, we shall learn, with
a brief study of Mary's rôle in each play, that the dramatists, while
building in general upon legend, were handling the theme of the

---

[1] *Ludus Coventriae, or The Plaie Called Corpus Christi,* London, 1922.
EETS. ES. 120, Introd., p. xx.

[2] *Op. cit.,* pp. 26-32.

[3] *Medieval Stage,* II, 126-127.

[4] *Op. cit.,* p. 82, *passim.*

[5] *Op. cit.,* Introd., p. xxxviii.

Mother of God in a way to carry the emphasis from the Mother to God. I mean that in the rôle there is more God than Mother.

THE CONCEPTION OF MARY

The first play of the Virgin Group is the one which Halliwell entitled the *Barrenness of Anna,* but which Miss Block preferred to label the *Conception of Mary.* These titles are mutually supplemental inasmuch as the play deals with the story of how Mary was conceived by a barren mother. Miss Block believes the play to be built upon the *Legenda Aurea,* while Parker contends that the author drew his material mainly from the *Life of St. Anne.* At any rate, the ecclesiastical spirit pervading the play testifies strongly to the probability that, like the rest of the Virgin Group, it was interwoven with, or at least undeniably influenced by what Miss Swenson calls " a very elaborate play which must undoubtedly be ecclesiastical in origin." [6] The following examples illustrate the ecclesiastical coloring, which is doubtless an excellent background for the character who is to be treated in her strictly theological status.

Joachim, first of all, is evidently represented as a priest, for after extolling the fact that he has distributed his patrimony in three parts, he adds:

> So xulde euery curat in þis werde wyde
> ʒeve a part to his chauncel i-wys
> A part to his parochonerys þat to povert slyde
> the thryd part to kepe for hym and his.

Possibly the author's [7] intent in representing Joachim as a " curat " was to echo the theme of Our Lord's sacerdotal, as well as regal descent, so apparent in the *Prophets* play. Other ecclesiastical tags appear in the stage direction:

> There they xal synge þis sequens Benedicta
> sit beata trinitas

---

[6] *Op. cit.,* p. 35.

[7] I would have it noted that whenever I allude to an author or dramatist, I allude only to the author of the play under study. I do not imply that one dramatist need be author of any other of the plays in the cycle. The authorship of the various plays, or groups of plays, throughout the cycles is a question outside the scope of the present study.

and in the prayers of *Ministro* and his staff:

> Adiutorium nostrum in nomine Domine
> Qui fecit . . .
> Sit nomen Domini benedictum
> Ex hoc . . .
> Benedicat vos diuina maiestas et vna deitas
>   Pater . . . Amen.

concluding with the rubric:

> Signando manu cum cruce solenniter et recedant tribus extra templum.

Besides these liturgical traces we further notice, as Kretzmann has so carefully demonstrated,[8] that the story of this play was already in the Sarum *lectiones* for St. Anne's Day, all of the principal characters being included: Anna, Joachim, Ysachar, *Pastores* and *Angelus,* with the sequence of events identical.

In a setting such as this we should hardly expect other than a Christocentric interpretation of the Mother of God. Reference to Mary in this play is of course rather slight, quite as we should expect at this stage of the group. However, where attention is centered upon her she becomes a means to an end—the end being Christ; and although surrounded by apocryphal material, nothing is said or done that militates in the slightest against her theological status.

Contemplacio, after opening the play (or rather, the whole group of plays, as his words would indicate) with a prayer that Christ conserve the congregation from perils past, present and to come, forecasts the real nature of Mary's rôle by announcing that

> This matere here mad is of þe *modyr of mercy.*

Anne, among her very first lines, clearly sounds the Christocentric note when she says:

> my name is Anne þat is to sey grace
> we wete not how gracyous god wyl to us be
> A *woman xulde bere cryst þese profecyes haue we*
> If god send frute and it be a mayd childe
> with all reuerens I vow to his mageste
> *sche xal be here foot mayd to mynyster here most mylde.*

---

[8] *Op. cit.,* p. 157, 159.

Angelus echoes a similar strain. He announces the good news to the melancholy Joachim:

> . . . Anne þi blyssyd wyff
> sche xal bere a childe xal hygth mary
> *whiche xal be blyssyd in here body and haue joys ffyff* [9]
> *and ful of þe holy goost inspyred syngulyrly*
> Sche xal be offryd in to þe temple solemply
> þat of here non evyl ffame xuld sprynge thus
> And as sche xal be bore of a barrany body
> So of here xal be bore with-out nature Jhesus
>   þat xal be savyour
> . . . vnto al man-kende

Angelus also tells Anne that she shall bear a child

> Whiche xal hyght mary and *mary xal bere jhesus*
> Which xal be savyour of all þe werd and us

And Anne, transported with joy, exclaims:

> I am so joyful I not what I may say
> Þer can no tounge telle what joye in me is
> I to bere a childe þat xal bere all mannys blys

It is apparent that the emphasis given Mary in this play comes only in virtue of her prerogative of " modyr of mercy." The teaching of the Catholic Church is that all Mary's prerogatives flow out of her supreme prerogative of Mother of God. And of course the thoroughly Catholic medieval mind knew this doctrine quite as well as any other doctrine of the Church.[10] Hence, although the *Conception of Mary* is built around an apocryphal story, Mary's rôle does not depart from the strict theological notion of her. She is constantly alluded to as Mother of Christ. Her rôle is purely Christocentric.

It is very conceivable that this play, offering as it does a fertile opportunity for discussion upon the immaculate conception of Mary, deliberately omits that theme in order not to hazard anything that might compromise the strict theological status of the Mother of God. The controversy which raged on the Continent

---

[9] Kretzmann, p. 161, points out several of the traditional interpretations placed upon the theme of Mary's Joys.

[10] For pertinent information on the medieval devotional attitude toward Mary, see Vernet, *Medieval Spirituality*, pp. 98-106.

concerning Mary's freedom from original sin was not lost in England.[11] Possibly the playwright (as the ecclesiastical tone of the play suggests) was a priest, or religious, of the opinion of those who opposed the doctrine. He seems, however, to make some concession to the Virgin's surpassing purity when he has *Angelus* inform Joachim that Anne shall bear a child

> which xal be blyssyd in here body and haue joys ffyff
> and ful of þe holy goost inspyred syngulyrly.

It is just possible, however, that the play may really be a tribute to the active conception of Mary, its author knowing nothing as yet of the fact (even St. Bernard and practically all the disputants of the day were unaware of it) that the doctrine applies only to her passive conception.[11a] In the unorthodox sense it would mean an ancestral transmission of immaculateness; hence the homage would have to extend to Saints Joachim and Anne, and even to their ancestors. This is exactly what St. Bernard feared in his famous letter (Epist. XLXXIV) when he remarked that "such a frequency of festivals is fit only for heaven, and not for this land of exile." I say it is just possible that the playwright may have had this wrong notion, and may have believed that by centering a play around the story of Anne and Joachim's joy in conceiving Mary, and by involving Mary as much as mere allusion would permit, he was thus honoring her conception.[12] All this is pure supposition, however, and I prefer to believe that the playwright, in assembling his piece, chose to remain entirely aloof from the controversy rather than to introduce anything at all liable to impair the pure Christocentric status of Mary, which he wished to portray.

[11] Cf. *ibid.*, pp. 103-104; also, Holweck, " The Immaculate Conception of the B. V. M.," in *Catholic Encyclopedia*, XII (1913), 675-687.

[11a] The active conception refers to the act of the parents, whereas the passive conception denotes the moment when the soul and body of the Virgin united. See further, W. Reany, *The Creation of the Human Soul*, pp. 197-198.

[12] To this day the Greek Church has a feast of the *Conception of St. Anne. Ibid.*, p. 677.

Mary in the Temple

With the present play Mary for the first time in Coventry comes upon the stage. The author is notably exact in maintaining the strict, essential note of her rôle, even amid the most apocryphal and elaborate dramatic surroundings. The play begins with a brief review of the preceding story by *Contemplacio,* who again invokes Mary with

> now þe modyr of mercy in þis be our sped.

Mary, a child of three, is led to the temple to be offered to the Lord in fulfillment of her parents' vow. For the first time we hear Anne address her, and her words are fraught with reference to the real status of the future Mother of God:

> Dowtere, þe Aungel tolde us ȝe xulde be a qwen
> Wole ȝe go se þat lord ȝour husbond xal ben
> and lerne for to love hym and lede with hym ȝour lyff
> telle ȝour ffadyr and me her ȝour answere let sen
> Wole ȝe be pure maydyn and also goddys wyff.

Before explaining the Christocentric note in these lines, I should like to point out another interesting feature. Anne quotes the angel of the previous play as having said that Mary would be a queen. But as a matter of fact, *Angelus* said no such thing in either of his apparitions. Why, then, the misquotation? I think the matter is easily explained if we reflect that the author himself must have been aware of the inaccuracy, but must also have held himself excused for two reasons: first, the idea of queenship has ever been a devotional appendage to Mary's title of Mother of God;[13] second (and here becomes apparent the alternate aim of the playwright—the showing forth of Mary's divine motherhood), the use of " queen " supplies a well-manipulated dramatic device, for our author uses it to attach the meaning of marriage to an earthly " lord," at the same time subtly hinting at its higher meaning—Mary's becoming Mother of God and Spouse of the Holy Ghost. This latter expression, " Spouse of the Holy Ghost," is the

---

[13] The playwright again employs this idea of queenship later on in the play when *Angelus,* in his acrostic to the name of Mary, says:
> R.   Regina of regyon Reyneng with-owtyn ende.

precise meaning of " Goddys wyff." It is simply the Catholic view-
point of Mary's status after giving her consent to become Mother
of God. Catholics believe, according to the article of faith as expressed in the Apostle's Creed, that Jesus Christ was conceived by
the Holy Ghost (". . . *Qui conceptus est de Spiritu Sancto* . . .").
And since in Mary this conception took place, her title of " Goddys
wyff," Spouse of the Holy Ghost, is thereby merited. Hence it was
unquestionably to her quality of Virgin Mother of God that our
author was alluding with the line:

> Wole 3e be pure maydyn and also goddys wyff.

Furthermore, Mary's answer verifies this interpretation:

> Ffadyr and modyr if it plesyng to 3ow be
> 3e han mad 3our a-vow so sothly wole I
> to be goddys chast seruaunt whil lyff is in me
> but to be goddys wyff I was nevyr wurthy
> I am þe symplelest þat evyr was born of body
> I haue herd 3ow seyd God xulde haue a modyr swete
> þat I may leve to se hire god graunt me for his mercy
> and Abyl me to ley my handys vndyr hire fayr fete.[13a]

The York *Annunciation*[14] play also refers to Mary as " Godis
spouse."

The significance of these first lines of Anne to her daughter continues further. The lines

> telle 3our ffadyr and me her 3our answere let sen
> Wole 3e be pure maydyn and also goddys wyff

indicate that our playwright had the orthodox view of Mary's status
as *voluntary* Mother of the Redeemer. Coventry seems insistent on
this point, although none of the other cycles touches upon it anywhere. The theme is repeated in the *Salutation and Conception*[15]

[13a] It is interesting to note the similarity between the last line of this
quotation and a line in Shakespeare's *Taming of the Shrew*, V, ii, 176-179.
Says the reformed Katharina:

> Then vail your stomachs, for it is no boot,
> And place your hands below your husband's foot:
> In token of which duty, if he please,
> My hand is ready, may it do him ease.

[14] Y. MS No. 12.   [15] C. MS No. 11.

wherein the conversation between Gabriel and Mary contains a
very apparent note of suspense until the Virgin's consent is gained.
She is even made to pause and consider the angel's proposal, according to the stage direction: " Here the aungel makyth a lytyl
restynge, and Mary beholdyth hym . . ." The climax approaches
when Gabriel, pressing her more and more for her consent, recalls
the longing of both the blessed in Heaven and the expectant in
limbo for the Saviour's coming. His last exhortation is much
to the point:

> As Adam Abraham and davyd in fere
> And many othere of good reputacion
> Þat þin Answere desyre to here
> and þin Assent to þe incarnacion
> In which þou standyst As persevere
> of All man-kende savacion
> Gyff me myn Answere now lady dere
> to All these creaturys comfortacion.

And when Mary accedes, Gabriel is profuse in his thanks. All this
dramatic intensity tends to emphasize the fact that Mary became
Mother of God entirely of her own volition. That Coventry should
stress this theme, while the other cycles ignore it, may serve to
bear out Miss Swenson's theory that a previous large Virgin play,
ecclesiastical in origin, forms the main texture of the Coventry
Mary Group.[16]

Returning to *Mary in the Temple,* I say there can be no doubt
that at times the author is adapting his story, though not obtru-
sively, to useful bits of didacticism. There are indications that this
play is the work of a man acquainted with at least one aspect of
convent life, the danger to which fervent but inexperienced novices
may expose themselves by over-mortification in food habits. *Episcopus,* informing Mary of the dispositions of mind required of
her in the Temple, does not fail to add that she must have " a
reasonable tyme to fede." A little further on in the same play,
Ysakar's servant, bringing food to Mary, says substantially,
" Ysakar bids you feed well and spare not, for now is a time for
meat and no longer for reading." If the dramatist were a religious
we should well understand why Mary's rôle receives such a promi-

[16] *Op. cit.,* p. 30.

nent Christocentric coloring. These allusions to convent life, however, are only accidental to the play; they do not compose its
theme. They are just another instance of the author's alertness
to a chance whereby to bring a brief and pleasant lesson before the
audience. Thus we again hear him telling us, with Joachim:

> Sche is so gracyous she is so mylde
> so xulde childyr to fadyr and modyr evyr more.

The play lists seven petitions of the Virgin as they occur in one
of her prayers. These petitions of Mary are identical with those in
Meditationes Vitae Christi and Lydgate's *Lyf of Our Lady,* with
the exception that the petition placed fifth in these two works is
placed last in the play and given a whole stanza—" an arrange-
ment," says Vriend, " which was no doubt suggested to the author
by his wish to lay special stress on it : "

> The sefnte Lord I haske with grett ffere
> Þat I may se onys in my lyve
> Þat lady þat xal goddys sone bere
> Þat I may serve here with my wyttys fyve
> If it plese ȝow . . .

This is clearly an effort to emphasize the Virgin's humility, by
setting it in the shadow of her future dignity of Mother of God.
The author is reiterating the idea he put so beautifully into Mary's
mouth at the beginning of the play:

> I haue herd ȝow seyd God xulde haue a modyr swete
> þat I may leve to se hire God graunt me for his mercy
> and Abyl me to ley my handys vndyr hire fayr fete.

The Betrothal of Mary

Chronologically this play naturally follows the preceding. Even
in regard to the *mise en scène* there is agreement. Both occur in
the temple. Although the York and Towneley cycles treat only
incidentally of the marriage of Mary and Joseph, Coventry uses
the theme for a distinct and even lengthy play. This is the third
play of the Coventry Virgin Group. Joseph is really the central
character. Mary's rôle, save for a moderate space at the beginning
and end, is for the most part passive. The story is simple. Mary
has reached the age wherein all Jewish maidens are obliged by law

to present themselves for marriage. Accordingly Joachim and Anne proceed to lead their daughter to the temple for " a spowse to wedde," because they cannot go " a-ȝen þe lawe." The high priest, Ysakar, welcomes the three and reminds Mary that she must select a spouse and thus fulfill the law. Mary's answer carries the theme of practically all that she says throughout the play:

> A-ȝens þe lawe wyl I nevyr be
> but mannys ffelachep xal nevyr folwe me
> I wyl levyn evyr in chastyte
> be þe grace of goddys wylle.

Ysakar is hugely perplexed at this extraordinary attitude and demands an explanation. Mary recalls the vow her parents had made in which they promised to give their child entirely up to the exclusive service of the Lord, and her own vow to consecrate herself in chastity to God. Ysakar is even more perplexed, wavering between the law of the Jews and the sacred obligations of a vow. In this quandary he is directed by the Lord to summon all the kinsmen of David to the temple, and there to make an offering of white rods. The owner of the rod which shall blossom will be he whom the Lord has chosen for Mary's spouse. Joseph, represented here as an old and feeble man, goes reluctantly and with difficulty to the temple with his kinsmen, and after much hesitation and stubbornness, presents his rod with the others, when lo! it blossoms. The scene which follows is painfully comical.[17] Ysakar is constrained to use every argument available to induce Joseph to wed the Virgin, but Joseph protests that he is old, feeble, etc., that it does not become an old man to take a young wife, that he has ever been a " maiden " and intends to remain so:

> I am an old man so god me spede
> and with a wyff now to levyn in drede
> It wore neyther sport nere game . . .
> An old man may nevyr thryff
> With a ȝonge wyff so god me saue.

---

[17] Were Joseph at that time the figure he is in the Church today, it is inconceivable that he should have been so dramatized. Not until toward the end of the fifteenth century did the St. Joseph cultus begin to spread in Europe. See Souvay, " St. Joseph," in *Catholic Encyclopedia,* VIII (1913), 506 ff.

Finally he submits to "the will of God" and agrees to wed Mary, stipulating, however, that they live forever in chastity, to which Mary of course is most willing, on account of her own vow. A very elaborate ceremony takes place, strongly suggestive of ecclesiastical coloring. Afterwards Joseph announces to his wife that, since he has not as yet a house of his own for them to live in, he will therefore go and order things as well as his means will allow. It is noteworthy here that, commenting on his poverty, he says to Mary:

> he þat is and evyr xal be
> Of hefne and helle Ryche kynge
> in erth hath chosyn poverte
> and all Ryches and welthis refusynge.

In other words, Joseph is anticipating the birth of Christ, or, as the less sympathetic of us might put it, the necessary sequence of time is being violated. However we cannot suppose that the medieval audience complained at such a pious and appropriate violation. Three maidens are given the holy couple as a protection against slanderous tongues.

These circumstances will better enable us to understand the words of Mary as they occur in the play. As I said before, the whole import of her words is her desire to live in chastity. Now nothing could be more expressive of her Christological status. This may sound a trifle sweeping at first, since the apocryphal gospels are quite unanimous in declaring Mary's desire to live chastely. On the stage, however, at least in the present instance, we discern something more than a mere reproduction of the apocrypha. It is well to bear in mind that no Catholic ever thought or thinks of Mary's prerogative of Mother of God apart from her virginity. That is why her virginity is so amply stressed in this play. It is why in the previous play, for instance, so much emphasis was laid upon her quality of "pure maydyn and also Goddys wyff." Likewise in the *Prophets* already discussed, Mary is never alluded to apart from her virginity, and the prophecy of Isaias, "Behold, a virgin shall conceive, and bear a son," receives a very apparent emphasis which can in no wise be explained except by the universal Catholic attitude towards Mary as virgin mother of Christ. I think the following observation from the play itself will bear out the point I am striving to explain. As soon as Joseph comes upon the scene, Mary merges into the background. She has merely stated her intention to remain a virgin, and now the brunt of comedy and burlesque falls upon Joseph. When Mary is reintroduced, her words are as sedate and edifying as ever; she reaffirms her desire for virginity, praises God and delights her soul with scriptural reading. But if the author's intent were merely to reproduce the apocrypha, and to exploit Mary simply as a dramatic figure, then why did he handle her with such delicacy and reserve? Just as the author of the Wakefield *Noe* play makes Noe share much of the comedy with his wife, why should not our author too transfer to Mary some of the comic excitement and ridiculous obstinacy of Joseph, a dramatic foil that even a medieval playwright must have sensed? Certainly there is no obstacle to such behaviour on her part, at least as far as the material of the story is concerned. Mary made a vow of virginity; then why did she not recalcitrate just as loudly and comically as Joseph, who was merely disinclined to marriage? Here indeed was plenty of scope for dramatic exploitation; still, Mary is gently drawn aside to make room for the quasi-buffoonery of Joseph. This reserve and delicacy in the Virgin's rôle indicates but one thing: She is looked upon only in her character of Mother of God. Nothing at all disrespectful to that character can be introduced—not even a word or gesture that might pass as an allowable "type" action. Nothing that is not edifying, nothing of the swagger of *Episcopus,* of the grumbling of Joseph, or of the self-complacency of the kinsmen of David escapes her prayerful lips. In the midst of absurdity and ridiculous excitement she alone remains as we should expect of the Mother of God—and as the devout people of the Middle Ages must have expected of her.

There is another feature of this play, taken as a whole, which further demonstrates that Mary's rôle refers to her character of Mother of God. This feature also proves to some extent that, however fine a story her marriage might make in itself, it is given a higher meaning. To come to the point at once, I shall quote the stanza from a later Coventry play, *Christ Disputing in the Temple*,[18] wherein one of the Doctors asks Jesus:

[18] C. MS No. 21.

> What nede was it here to be wedde
> On to A man of so grett Age
> lesse þan þei myght bothe ago to bedde
> and kept þe lawe of maryage.

That is to say (and the thought must have occurred to many a reader of both canonical and apocryphal gospels) why should the couple have married at all when both intended to live in perpetual chastity? Jesus in the play referred to, answers the question:

> To blynde þe devyl of his knowlache
> and my byrth from hym to hyde
> þat holy wedlok was grett stopage
> þe devyl in dowte to do A-byde.
> Also whan sche xulde to egypte gon
> and fle from herowde for dowte of me
> be-cawse sche xulde nat go Alon
> Joseph was ordeyned here make to be
> my ffadyr of his hyȝ mageste
> here for to comforte in þe way
> these be þe cawsys as ȝe may se
> why joseph weddyd þat holy may.

This answer, as far as it goes, is exactly similar to the reasons advanced by St. Jerome and Origen.[19] Vriend notes, too, that this answer is the common one in the theological writings of the time.[20]

The allusions to the marriage of Mary and Joseph in York and Towneley are essentially the same as the story in Coventry. It is only this latter cycle that saw fit to accord it a separate play. And Mary's part in that play has demonstrated clearly enough that hers is a purely Christological rôle, and that despite the wide scope of dramatic possibilities this rôle offers, she is made to act strictly in the light of her divine maternity.

THE SALUTATION AND CONCEPTION

Unlike the theme of the play we have just examined, the story of the Annunciation, contained in all four cycles, is woven faithfully upon the canonical account of Matthew, I, 26-46. The Virgin's status of Mother of Christ is very much stressed in all of the plays. Coventry introduces the story with an account of the

---

[19] Cf. Livius, *op. cit.*, pp. 121-122.   [20] *Op. cit.*, p. 60.

Parliament of Heaven, a medieval mystical theme, very appropriate as a prologue to the Annunciation story.[21] This theme easily lends itself to dramatization, as is plainly seen in Coventry. The characters of the *Parliament* are *Pater, Filius, Spiritus Sanctus, Pax, Justicia, Misericordia, Veritas* and *Virtutes.* A lively discussion is provoked among all by the supplication of *Virtutes:*

> Lord plesyth it þin hyȝ domynacion
> On man þat þou made to haue pyte
> Patryarchys and prophetys han made supplycacion
> oure offyse is to presente here prayerys to the
> Aungelys Archaungelys we thre
> þat ben in þe fyrst ierarchie
> Ffor man to þin hy mageste
> Mercy mercy mercy we crye.

The *Virtutes* go on to beseech for mercy upon fallen mankind, that he may be restored to his fellowship with the angels. *Veritas* and *Justicia* object to such leniency, while the others second the prayer of *Virtutes.* At last the Lord decides to send redemption to men. The Trinity immediately holds a council. *Filius* volunteers to shoulder the burden of redemption and the council amicably ends. *Gabryel* is deputed by *Pater* to announce the mystery to the Virgin in Nazareth:

> The name of þe mayd ffre
> Is Mary þat xal Al Restore.

Filius adds:

> Say þat she is with-owte wo and ful of grace
> And þat I þe son of þe godhed of here xal be bore
> Hyȝe þe þou were there A pace
> ellys we xal be there the be-ffore
> I haue so grett hast to be man thore

---

[21] Cf. Pollard, *English Miracle Plays, Moralities and Interludes* (5th ed., Oxford, 1909), pp. 224b-224c. A comprehensive essay on this theme has been written by Miss Hope Traver, *The Four Daughters of God*, Bryn Mawr Dissertation, 1907. See also Hemingway, *English Nativity Plays,* New York, 1909, " Notes on the Coventry Annunciation play." Pollard, *loc. cit.*, p. 224c, notes that " there are numerous references to this colloquy in heaven in writers of the fifteenth century, and it forms the subject of one of the pictures in some of the French editions of the *Hours of the Blessed Virgin,* which often illustrate the Miracle Plays."

> In þat mekest and purest virgyne
> Sey here she xal restore
> Of ȝow Aungellys þe grett Ruyne.

And *Spiritus Sanctus* enjoins:

> And if she Aske þe how it myth be
> telle here I þe holy gost xal werke al this
> Sche xal be savyd thorwe oure vnyte . . .
> Here body xal be so ful-fylt with blys
> Þat she xal sone thynke þis sownde credyble.

These lines adequately show what dignified proportion the mystery assumes and how thoroughly reverent is the merest reference to Mary. Everything here is a tribute to her prerogative. I shall show later that the play as a whole in Coventry is an effort to extol the fact that Mary voluntarily became Mother of God. Many things would indicate this; and whereas in the other cycles the Annunciation is treated as an episode along with one or more stories, in Coventry it exists as a distinct play.

In regard to this play there is throughout all four cycles a common theme at the outset, namely, the fall of man. Towneley develops it most fully, and although it nowhere bears directly upon Mary it nevertheless serves as a solemn prologue, so to speak, to her entry into the play. It forecasts the magnitude of her rôle as co-operatrix in the Redemption.[22]

Quite as Scripture indicates, Mary is frightened at the vision of an angel showering unheard-of praises upon her. Only in Coventry does she voice a reason for her alarm:

> A mercy god þis is a marvelyous herynge
> In þe Aungelys wordys I am trobelyd her
> I thynk how may be þis gretynge
> Aungelys dayly to me doth Aper
> But not in þe lyknes of man þat is my fer

---

[22] Cf. with the Annunciation homily of St. Gregory Thaumaturgus: " . . . The tenor of his message was as follows: I am moved by my compassion to descend to earth in order to recover the lost Adam. Sin has made him to destroy who was made to my image, and hath corrupted the work of my hands, and obscured the beauty which I formed. Go therefore to the Virgin Mary . . ." in Livius, *The Blessed Virgin in the Fathers of the First Six Centuries*, p. 123.

And Also thus hyȝly to comendyd be
and am most vn-wurthy I can-not Answere
grett shamfastnes and grett dred is in me.

Coventry above all wishes to stress the reality of her divine motherhood. After consenting to the Angel's proposal she announces that the incarnation has already taken place within her, and that the Child is immediately endowed with all His limbs:

A now I ffele in my body be
parfyte god and parfyte man
havyng Al schappe of chyldly carnalyte
Evyn Al at onys þus god be-gan.[23]

And in his lines of farewell Gabriel says:

Ffare wel goddys modyr I þe honowre
Ffare wel goddys sustyr . . .
Ffare wel goddys chawmere and his bowre.
I comende me on to ȝow þou trone of þe trinyte
O mekest mayde now þe modyr of jhesu . . .
Thour ȝour body beryth þe babe oure blysse xal renew
to ȝow modyr of mercy most mekely I recomende
and as I began I ende with An Ave new
Enjonyd hefne and erth . . .

It is readily seen from these lines alone that the Virgin's rôle is entirely contributory to the glorifying of her Son.

All the dramatists in dealing with this theme have omitted a very pertinent episode, mentioned in the apocrypha (*Protev.* XI; *Pseudo-Matthew* IX), in which Mary receives a preliminary salutation at the fountain. Just why our dramatists should omit the story may possibly be explained on the assumption that they considered the theme of the play too exalted for such embroidery. The apocryphal notion would not harmonize with the Virgin's rôle here. The Annunciation was too sacred, I think it safe to say, too

---

[23] There can be no doubt that the dramatist adopts this idea as a means to heighten the effect of her actually being the mother of the incarnate Word. It serves to glorify that prerogative, just as does the idea of her not experiencing any of the pains of maternity, as indicated in the line:

With-owte peyne in Fflesche and bon

This painless birth idea regarding Mary is taught both by St. Augustine (Serm. 215) and St. Zeno (see Migne, *P. L.* XI, 413-417).

momentous to the mind of the dramatist and his audience to receive an uncanonical fringe, however interesting. Of course it is impossible to determine whether this is the exact reason why the fringe is rejected. At all events, it does not appear anywhere in the cycles. Considering that apocryphal notions are frequently incorporated in other plays, it would seem inexplicable that the dramatists omitted this highly dramatic feature otherwise than designedly; and if designedly, the only logical reason appears to be that they deemed it incompatible with the loftiness of the theme, and the corresponding loftiness that should characterize the Virgin's rôle. There is also a possibility that the incident was not widely enough known. Nevertheless, we find it recorded in the Late Old English translation of *Pseudo-Matthew* (*Bibl. AS. Prosa,* III, 133) and the history of Joachim, Anna, and Mary in the Auchinleck MS. (ed. by W. B. Turnbull in *Legendae Catholicae,* p. 154). The Annunciation at the Spring has several iconographic representations, contained at present in (a) A Greek Gospel of the eleventh century, in the Bibliothèque Nationale, Paris; (b) Milan Cathedral, on ivory book covers; (c) S. Kensington, Victoria and Albert Museum, on an ivory casket.[24] I prefer to believe that we have here an instance of the rejection of dramatic material, in favor of preserving a reverent atmosphere.

Evidently then, there is no reason to question the character of Mary's rôle in the Coventry *Annunciation* play. Really the story in itself is rich in dramatic possibilities. If Mary were simply a detached dramatic figure, what could have checked the pen of the playwrights? Just as Joseph gave us some high entertainment, even when bidden by direct revelation to assume the noblest charge upon earth, why could not Mary have petulantly refused, stubbornly balked, and created some scenes when asked to assume a responsibility as tragic certainly to her as it was noble? On the contrary, we see only a rigid adherence to Gospel facts. Clearly the rôle of Mary was considered too lofty—even to the extent of excluding dramatically good apocryphal matter.[25]

[24] See E. B. Smith, *Early Christian Iconography,* Princeton, 1918.

[25] Likewise the *Pageant of the Shearmen and Taylors* of Coventry, having a complete Annunciation episode, adheres strictly to the Gospel account. See H. Craig, *Two Coventry Corpus Christi Plays.*

In the York, Towneley and Chester *Annunciation* play, no less than in Coventry, Mary's rôle is completely Christocentric. While the Gospel account is being enacted everything seems to be made to contribute to the honor of the Virgin's divine motherhood. It is not necessary to describe in detail all the factors in each play that evidence this Christocentricity; a few of the more salient lines will illustrate clearly enough. Thus in Towneley, when God is deputing Gabriel to Mary, He adds among other equally complimentary things:

> I haue hyr chosen, that madyn swete,
> She shall conceyf my derlying,
> Thrugh thy word and her herying.
> In hyr body wyll I lyght
> That is to me clenly dyght;
> She shall of hyr body bere
> God and man wythouten dere.
> She shall be blyssyd wythouten ende;
> Grayth the gabriell, and weynd.

Chester, which simply paraphrases the Gospel wording, nevertheless allows Mary modestly to direct attention to her supreme prerogative:

> Loe Gods chosen mekelie here!
> and lord god, prince of power,
> leeve that it fall in such manere
> this word that thou hast said.

York, aside from the Prologue, builds upon the Gospel wording so completely, that every stanza is a direct reference to Mary's status of Mother of the Saviour. Before attempting to show, as I promised, the fact that the Coventry *Annunciation* as a whole aims to emphasize Mary's volitional part in becoming Mother of Christ, I should like to bring together a few scattered particulars that further show the rôle of the Virgin to be purely Christocentric.

In the *Annunciation* Prologue of York, the prophet Amos explains again for us the interesting question of why the Mother of God married. His explanation is this: God willed Mary to be wed in order thus to deceive the fiend. Moreover, Christ would then arouse no suspicions either upon Himself or upon Mary, since wedlock would be a protective device:

So was the godhede closed and cledde
In wede of weddying whare thy wente . . .

The idea in these lines centering attention upon the fact that Mary married, even while intent upon remaining a virgin, has also come up in my discussion of the *Betrothal of Mary.* I have noted therein that the reason given for Mary's marriage (identical with the explanation of the prophet Amos), is derived almost exactly from the reason advanced by St. Jerome and Origen (Livius, 121-122). Towneley finds another method of emphasizing the divine motherhood by centering attention upon the parallel existing between Eve and Mary, the Fall and the Redemption. A man (Adam), a virgin (Eve), and an angel (the devil), were the chief actors on the scene of the downfall of mankind; but another Man (Christ), another Virgin (Mary), and another angel (Gabriel), bring salvation, and over against the death-dealing tree of Eden there rises the life-giving roodtree of Calvary:

ffor reson wyll that ther be thre,
A man, a madyn, and a tre:
Man for man, tre for tre,
Madyn for madyn; thus shal it be.[26]

Further on *Deus* addresses *Gabriel:*

Angell must to mary go,
ffor the feynd was eue fo;
He was foule and layth to syght,
And thou are angell fayr and bright;
And hayls that madyn, my lemman,
As heyndly as thou can.
Of my behalf thou shall hyr grete,
I have hyr chosen, that madyn swete . . .

Coventry, paraphrasing the Angelical Salutation, toys with the words *Ave* and *Eva:*

here þis name Eva is turnyd Aue
þat is to say with-owte sorwe are ȝe now.
Thow sorwe in ȝow hath no place
ȝett of joy lady ȝe nede more
Therfore I Adde And sey fful of grace

---

[26] The same analogy is found in Augustine, Maternus, Zeno, Gregory. Cf. Livius, 123-136.

To understand the symbolism in this contrast between the two words we should bear in mind that, according to the philology of the medieval cloister, the word " Ave " was composed of *a* privative and *ve,* that is *vae* (in English " woe "), so that by greeting Mary with " Ave," the reverse, the angel signified the contrast between the mother of woe and the mother of bliss. Thus Gabriel in Coventry is ordered to tell Mary " that she is withowte woe and ful of grace." All this comes, of course, of her status of Mother of the Redeemer.[27]

Just why the Coventry *Annunciation* play, taken as a whole, is meant to stress the volitional rôle of Mary in assuming the responsibility of Mother of the Saviour is not difficult to see. There is an evident narrative movement to this play, the climax coming with Mary's consent to become the instrument of the Incarnation. The *Parliament of Heaven* begins the piece and depicts the dire need of mankind for redemption. *Virtutes* in heaven, imploring mercy for the world, *ipso facto* starts the lengthy discussion by *Pater, Filius,* etc. upon the advisability of sending a Saviour to earth. The positive decision arrived at, there immediately occurs the question: By whom will the Saviour become incarnate? Mary is the choice. The intensity of emotion now shifts to this crucial point: Will she consent? I have already indicated, in my discussion upon *Mary in the Temple,* the dramatic intensity of this scene. Mary actually considers the tremendous meaning of the angel's proposal. Meanwhile Gabriel adduces reason after reason in pleading for her consent. And the crisis is over when she finally does consent. The play continues without interest from this point, with occasional " backward glances " at the dignity and generosity of the now-Mother of God. This scene is of course an adaptation of the traditional Christian teachings upon the topic. The Church frequently emphasizes this volitional act of Mary in order to show forth her supreme part in the sufferings of Christ and her status of coredemptrix.

In the twelfth and thirteenth centuries, Mary was honored above all as Mother of Mercy, Mother of Sinners; and it is owing to her

---

[27] Cf. Livius, 124. Also Gueranger, *The Liturgical Year* (*Advent*), Dublin, 1883, p. 204; and C. Brown, *Religious Lyrics of the XIV Century,* Oxford, 1916-1920, pp. 55 and 58.

volitional motherhood of the Redeemer that these titles were accorded her. [28] Indeed, we again catch the refrain later on in the Coventry *Assumption of the Virgin* wherein *Michael* says:

> Hefne and erthe now injoye may ye
> Ffor god throw mary is mad mannys frend.

Gabriel's parting words in the Coventry *Annunciation* are quite similar:

> Thour 3our body beryth þe babe oure blysse xal renew
> to 3ow modyr of mercy most mekely I recomende
> and as I began I ende—with An Ave new
> Enjonyd hefne and erth . . .

JOSEPH'S RETURN

We turn now to the dramatized story of Joseph's doubt and anxiety at finding his wife with child. It will testify clearly to what I have been trying to show regarding the rôle of Mary. Coventry and York developed the theme in separate plays, while Chester embodies it in the *Salutation and Nativity,* and Towneley in the *Annunciation.* We can discern in each cycle the dramatist's awareness of having in hand a story capable of almost limitless exploitation. Each dramatist has indeed done his task to a rather unpleasing degree of ruggedness. We must remember that the scriptural account of Joseph's trouble, besides being worded with the utmost delicacy, is decidedly brief. In the mysteries, however, this incident, with its apocryphal background (*Pseudo-Matthew*) is expanded into something perhaps rather bizarre to the modern reader. The unguarded bluntness of Joseph, who is laboring under deep emotional stress, his distraction at having married at all, his incessant grumbling and his exaggerated pleadings to know the truth, are very realistically pictured. But that the story found favor before the medieval audience is beyond question. In those days there was not the liturgical veneration for Joseph that is accorded him today. With medieval folk, that patriarch could be maltreated to the very limit so long as the dignity of Mary was not

---

[28] Regarding the early and medieval status of Mary as coredemptrix, see Vernet, *Medieval Spirituality,* p. 101; also *Blickling Homilies of the Tenth Century,* I, p. 9, ed. by Morris, EETS. OS. 58 (1874).

impaired.[29] I shall show how deftly Mary is spared in this story as it occurs in the cycle, and how the delicate handling of her rôle turns upon her dignity of Mother of the Christ. Furthermore we can discern in this grotesquerie of Joseph a bit of the medieval relish for comedy, especially of the cuckold husband type.[30]

I have called the treatment of this story rugged, and it assuredly is in places. But for this reason we cannot *de facto* attribute a coarse or irreverent mind, either to the various playwrights or to the folk who must have attended the presentation in crowds.[31]

Although in general the cycles differ in dramatizing the story of Joseph's return, yet in several points they agree. In all the plays, Joseph's great concern consists in exonerating himself and demanding of Mary who the father of the Child is.[32] And in two of the plays Mary repeats several times that the Child she bears is both God's and his own; thus in *Coventry:*

Joseph:	Sey me Mary þis childys fadyr ho is
	I pray þe telle me and þat anon
Maria:	The fadyr of hevyn and ȝe it is
	other fadyr hath he non
	I dede nevyr forfete with man i-wys
	Wher-fore I pray ȝow amende ȝour mon
	this childe is goddys and ȝour.

This answer provokes mingled fear and anger in the grief-stricken Joseph. It would seem that he takes it for an attempt on Mary's part to incriminate him. He insistently proclaims his innocence, makes dark allusions to whoever is father of the Child, and continues to plead with Mary for the truth. Only in York does he

[29] The theme is likewise developed in the *Pageant of the Shearmen and Taylors of Coventry.* Cf. *Two Coventry Corpus Christi Plays, op. cit.*

[30] " . . . the humorous treatment of Joseph in the Corpus Christi Plays . . . may, in fact, be due to the eternal ridiculing of old men with young wives in the semi-religious lyrics." (Taylor, " The Relation of the English Corpus Christi Play to the Middle English Religious Lyric," in *Modern Philology*, V (1907), No. 1, p. 7).

[31] See, in this connection, Hone's *Ancient Mysteries Described*, London, 1823, p. 220; also Brother Azarias, *Essays Miscellaneous*, Chicago, 1896, pp. 25-26.

[32] Cf. Woodward, *The Most Holy Mother of God in the Songs of the Eastern Church*, London, 1919, p. 37.

expressly state the reason for his alarm at Mary's avowal that the
Child is his own:

> Therfore, telle me in priuite
> whos is þe childe þou is with nowe?
> Sertis, þer sall non witte but we,
> I drede þe law als wele as þou.

In none of these plays does Joseph challenge Mary's purity.
He intimates, of course, that she has wronged him, but immediately turns the topic more upon himself. His own wretched-
ness, his lament at having ever married, his wrath at whoever is
father of the Child—these come into the limelight, but not the
criminality of Mary, even for a dramatic instant. This turning of
attention from Mary to Joseph is evident in all four plays. Ob-
viously the dramatists are deliberately refraining from exploiting
the fact of Mary's pregnancy. The dramatic outlet is found
entirely in Joseph. The emotion and excitement of the event fall
upon him. The Virgin Mary, however, seems drawn as much as
possible into the background.

In Towneley, Coventry and York, Mary's virgins are doubtless
introduced primarily to impress both upon Joseph and upon the
spectators the pure seclusion in which she must have lived while her
spouse was away. Of course they also serve as interesting dramatic
devices; in Coventry for instance, Susanna's zeal for the seclusion
of her mistress prompts her to challenge even the returning Joseph.
In Towneley the virgins are merely alluded to by Joseph in his
troubled soliloquy, in which he accuses them of trying to shield
Mary when they say that only an angel visited her during his
absence. York uses them to affirm before Joseph the innocence of
his wife, that her only intercourse was with angels, and that her
Child was conceived by the Holy Ghost. In all three plays, we discern the author's intent to heighten by every means possible the
virginity and miraculous conception of Mary. It is the only dramatic treatment that he appears willing to accord her. A restraint,
ascribable only to a popular reverence to the Virgin as Mother of
Christ, holds further dramatization in check — despite the rich
opportunities the story naturally offers.

But the most telling proof of Mary's Christocentric status here
is to be found in her own words. Although the play by its very

nature would seem to call primarily for a vindication of her
virginity, we find, nevertheless, that this aspect is almost totally
neglected in favor of acclaiming that the Child in her womb is
Jesus, God, the Expected of Nations.   See, for instance, in
Coventry:

Maria: It is no man but swete jhesus
he wyll be clad in flesch and blood
and of ȝour wyff be born.
Ffor sothe þe Aungel þus seyd he
þat goddys sone in trynite
Ffor mannys sake a man wolde be
To save þat is for-lorn.

and in York:

Maria: Joseph, yhe ar begiled,
With synne was I neuer filid,
Goddis sande is on me sene . . .
Sertis, it is Goddis sande,
Þat sall I never go fra . . .
Now, grete God! be you wisse,
And mende you of your mysse,
Of me, what so betyde.
Als he is kyng of blysse,
Sende yhou som seand of þis,
In truth þat ye might bide.

In both Chester and Towneley, Joseph merely grieves to himself
at finding his spouse with child.   In Towneley, Mary speaks only a
few words toward the end, in which she freely forgives her re-
pentant spouse.   And in every case *Angelus* informs Joseph that
the Child in Mary's womb is God, conceived of the Holy Ghost.
This scriptural finish overwhelms the relieved man with gratitude
to God for entrusting the Divine Child to his care.

Again, in Towneley, we espy Joseph withdrawing from his wife
not out of selfishness, as depicted in the other cycles, but solely
through a motive of his own unworthiness: [33]

[33] It is noteworthy that the dialogue between Mary and Joseph here is
very similar to that employed by the Fathers on the subject.   Athanasius,
for instance, also conceives of a conversation between the holy pair in which
Mary, reproached by her chagrined spouse, states that angels, shepherds
and kings will convince him of her innocence (Migne, *P. G.* 28, pp. 951 ff.).

> And sothly, if it so befall,
> Godys son that she be with all,
> If sich grace myght betyde,
> I wote well that I am not he,
> which that is worthi to be
> That blyssed body besyde,
> Nor yit to be in company;
> To wyldernes I will for thi
> Enfors me for to fare

At one moment in York the thought crosses Joseph's mind that his wife may be the Virgin foretold in prophecy, who is to give birth to the promised Messiah; but he relinquishes the idea at once:

> But wele I wate thurgh prophicie,
> A maiden clene suld bere a childe,
> But it is nought sho . . .

It is clear that Mary's part, malleable as is the story containing it, admits of nothing compromising to her status of Mother of God. We have seen that Joseph's accusation, necessary as it is to the play, is decidedly softened. The high emotional excitement natural to such a story devolves wholly upon Joseph, and Mary is spared as much as possible. In Chester and Towneley a marked delicacy prevails, the whole of the piece being embodied in Joseph's monologue, to the exclusion of Mary. Nowhere in all four cycles is Mary's vow of virginity aspersed; and instead of vindicating her innocence, as we should expect, she is wholly intent upon proclaiming that she bears in her womb the Son of God.

Chrysostom, depicting Mary's grief at Joseph's suspicions, makes her exclaim: *Ubi nunc es, qui mihi, Ave gratia plena, dixisti?* (*P. G.* 60, pp. 758 ff.). In the version of Proclus (*P. G.* 65, pp. 736 ff.), Mary addresses Joseph: *Crede jam radicem Jesse ultro germinasse immarcescibilem florem vitae.* And Germanus shows the unhappy Joseph especially eager to know the father of the Child (*P. G.* 98, pp. 331 ff.). It is difficult to determine from this similarity whether the Coventry and York dramatists of this theme were conversant with the Fathers; still there can be no doubt that they had the general Patristic tradition. In Part I of *Cynewulf's Christ* there is likewise a dialogue between Mary and Joseph regarding the Virgin's condition. See: Burgert, *The Dependence of Part I of Cynewulf's Christ upon the Antiphonary*, p. 76.

THE VISIT TO ELIZABETH

The coarseness of *Joseph's Return* is missing from *The Visit to Elizabeth,* which finds a place in each of the cycles. Both Towneley and Coventry make a separate play of it. The most notable feature of this piece in all the cycles is its faithful adherence to the Gospel narrative (Luke I, 39-56). Coventry elaborates somewhat, introducing the story of Zachary's dumbness (Luke I, 5-25), and adds several very delightful home-touches that must have enlivened the affair for an audience already well informed upon the Gospel story. Mary requests Joseph to accompany her into Elizabeth's house, informing him that their cousin is with child. Joseph is happy at the news:

> A godys sake is she with childe sche
> than wole here husbond zakarye be mery.

Joseph then observes that their cousin lives fifty-two miles away, in "montana." [34] However, he acquiesces, "with a good wyl" and Mary urges that they hurry their journey, alleging

> ffor I am schamfast of þe pepyl to be seyne
> and namely of men þer of I am A-gast
> Pylgrymagys and helpyngys wolde be go in hast
> þe more þe body is peynyd þe more is þe mede

Then, characteristically, she adds:

> Say ʒe ʒour devocionys and I xal myn I cast
> now in þis jurny god mote us spede.

While the scene is shifting to Zachary's house, *Contemplacio* relates the story of Elizabeth's conception. Then we find ourselves with the two pilgrims directly outside the home of the old couple. From this point on, Mary's maternity is the central topic of discussion. Although the dramatist bases his work entirely upon the scriptural story, it is surprising that here, as well as in the *Annunciation* play, we do not find any dramatic extension outside of the slight touches I have already mentioned.

The Gospel story of Mary's visit to Elizabeth has filtered into many medieval writings and has formed an abiding theme for

[34] Here St. Luke's *abiit in montana* is apparently interpreted as the name of a place.

sculpture and painting. Writers sought to depict the humility and glory of Mary on this occasion, and painters and sculptors delighted to represent the two holy women embracing each other.[35] The Visitation existed as a feast as early as 1263.[36] These few facts demonstrate that our playwrights and medieval folk in general loved a New Testament theme even though it were not elaborated with apocrypha. With Davidson, I think that these themes as a whole, whether they belonged to scriptural or legendary categories, were fundamentally a matter of simple piety, of earnest devotion rather than material for the fancy of the dramatists.[37] Doubtless the mysteries in general must have appeared quite as simple to the medieval play-goer as they do to us today. But it was the mystical magnitude of their themes that meant more to the spectators than did all the structural plainness of the plays themselves.[38]

Returning to our play, then, we find it is scarcely more than a paraphrasing of St. Luke's brief account. Coventry and Towneley do try to touch up and round out the piece here and there. Before turning to the Towneley account I shall show how painstaking Coventry is to concentrate attention upon the fact of Mary's divine maternity;—even aside from the stress laid upon it in the Gospel narrative.

Mary enters the house and salutes Elizabeth. The latter's answer pays tribute to the Mother of God in a lyrical paraphrase of the Gospel:

> mekest mayden and þe modyr of god . . .
>   . . . to oure god reverently

---

[35] See Love, trans., *Mirrour of the Blessed Lyf of Jesu Christ*, London, 1908; *The Lytylle Childrenes Lytil Boke*, ed. Furnivall. EETS. OS. 32 (1868). For iconography upon the event, see Smith, *Early Christian Iconography*, Princeton, 1922, p. 224. The two women generally meet either clasping each other's arms, or not embracing at all.

[36] Cf. Holweck, "The Visitation of the B. V. M.," in *Catholic Encyclopedia*, XV (1913), 481.

[37] Cf. C. Davidson, *Studies in the English Mystery Plays*, Yale Dissertation, 1892.

[38] Taking the theme in question, we cannot say that the *Visitation* does not contain very forceful and beautiful, inherently dramatic elements. Few themes in all English literature offer as good. As it stands it hardly needs dramatic embellishment.

> whom ȝe bere in ȝour body . . .
> And blyssyd be þe frute of þi wombe also
> þou wurthyest virgyne and wyff þat evyr was wrought
> how is it þat þe modyr of god xulde come to
> þat wrecche of all wrecchis . . . [referring to herself.]

Mary's answer conveys the impression that her attention is directed
to God rather than to herself:

> To þe preysynge of god cosyn this seyd mut be
> whan I sat in my lytyl hous on to god praynge
> Gabryel come and seyde to me Ave
> ther I conceyvyd god At my consentynge
> Parfyte god and parfyte man At onys beynge

After Mary has finished the *Magnificat,* the two women resume
their conversation, which as usual centers upon the divine maternity.   When the Virgin offers to remain three months with her
cousin

> tyl ȝe han childe to wasche skore and swepe
> and in all þat I may to comforte ȝow,

Elizabeth answers:

> A ȝe modyr of god ȝe shewe us here how
> we xulde be meke þat wrecchis here be
> All hefne and herthe wurcheppe ȝow mow
> þat are trone and tabernakyl of þe hyȝ trinite

And toward the end of the play Elizabeth urges that both she and
her husband go immediately to the temple to thank the Lord for
the great event that is about to take place:

> þe tyme þat is comynge now
> ffor now is cum mercy and venjauns is past
> God wyl be born for mannys prow
> to brynge us to blysse þat euer xal last.

This play in Coventry ends what has been called the Virgin
Group.   If, as the general didactic and orthodox tone of this set
of plays would indicate, they were written by a monk or an ecclesias-
tic, then it is easy to understand why Mary's rôle in them should be
so thoroughly Christocentric.   Several interesting theories have
been advanced anent the origin of this Virgin Group in Coventry.
Swenson believes they comprise new plays interpolated into an old

group which was specially modified for the purpose.[39]   K. S. Block, the latest editor of *Ludus Coventriae,* sees in the Virgin Group a composite of two older cycles.[40]   And, while not disputing any of the foregoing theories, R. S. Parker contends that the plays are largely composed of material borrowed from the stanzaic *Life of St. Anne.*[41]   The *Visitation* of Coventry, while adding dramatic coloring to the Gospel episode, does not fail to introduce a bit of asceticism strongly suggestive of a preacher's pen, and occurring in the play when Joseph is informed of Zachary's muteness.   Addressing the afflicted man, he says:

> Of ȝour dissese thynkys no greff
> thank god of al aduersyte
> Ffor he wyl chastyse and repreff
> þo þat he lovyth most hertyle.

Furthermore, *Contemplacio* winds up the performance with an exposition of the origin of the Hail Mary (as much of it as was then in use),[42] and specifies the indulgence granted to those who for a year recite daily Our Lady's Psalter.

The Virgin is very reverently depicted.   Of course we have probably noticed by this time that the reverence accorded Mary in the plays we have discussed does not stifle the dramatic qualities that are inherently hers.   The dramatists have succeeded in depicting what all the world admires: a simple, guileless, gentle, pious maid.   We cannot imagine for a moment that the medieval man or woman allowed his or her reverence for Mary to obscure these lovely qualities.   Neither have the dramatists overlooked them.

Chester, aside from its *Magnificat,* which I shall discuss under the topic in general at the end of this chapter, offers no material for special comment, inasmuch as it is but a paraphrase of the Gospel narrative.   This, of course, is purely Christocentric, and in the play Mary is dramatized only in view of her great preroga-

[39] *An Inquiry into the Composition and Structure of Ludus Coventriae.*
[40] *Ludus Coventriae, or the Plaie Called Corpus Christ.*
[41] *Stanzaic Versions of the Life of St. Anne.*
[42] See Thurston, *Catholic Encyclopedia,* VII (1913), 110-112, for a scholarly discussion of the "Hail, Mary."

tive. In York the circumstances are about identical, although the author seems to have taken special pains to emphasize the divine motherhood, for he provides Mary with this lyrical utterance:

> Nowe lorde! blist be þou ay
> For þe grace þou has me lente;
> Lorde I lofe þe god verray,
> þe sande þou hast me sente.
>
> I þanke þe nyght and day,
> And prayes with goode entente
> þou make me to thy paye,
> To þe my wille is wentte.

The Towneley dramatist offers us a little more diversified material. Here, as in Coventry, the *Salutation of Elizabeth* is a separate play. Rather than broach the Gospel story at once, the author presents an extended scene of greeting between the two women. Mary salutes her cousin, discloses that she has long desired to speak to her, answers Elizabeth's queries concerning the health of Joachim and Anne; then suddenly without a note of transition, the story proper is plunged into; Elizabeth salutes the Virgin as Mother of God. Thenceforward the usual scene continues. After reciting the *Magnificat* Mary takes leave of her kinswoman, but not until the latter, in reverence of the Virgin's divine maternity, exacts a kiss of her:

> Wyll thou now go, godys fere?
> Com kys me, doghter, with good chere,
> or thou hens gang;
> ffarewell now, thou frely foode!
> I pray the be of comforth goode,
> ffor thou art full of grace;
> Grete well all oure kyn of bloode;
> That lord, that the with grace infude,
> he saue all in this place.

We have seen that each play, quite in accord with the Gospel account, terminates with a *Magnificat,* to which is appended, in Chester and Coventry, a *Gloria Patri.* Kretzmann has adduced this fact as a powerful proof of the liturgical connection of these plays:

The Visitation ends with a translation of the Gloria Patri. This Gloria

Patri in connection with the Magnificat establishes the connection of this play with the liturgy, the model before the author having been either the liturgy itself or a liturgical play taken from the services.[43]

A commentary upon this conclusion would be that undoubtedly the liturgy was at least the inspiration of the *Magnificat* insertion, since only the liturgical services contained this canticle in a fashion accessible to the minds of the laity. But a further observation would be, as Vriend has demonstrated [44] that in the case of Chester the *Magnificat* was altered from the Vulgate version (alone of liturgical usage) into that adopted by Erasmus in his Latin translation of the New Testament. This appears in the Latin marginal notes accompanying an English paraphrase of the canticle. In addition, we discover the Towneley author blundering over Latin. In the passage, " suscepit Israel puerum suum " (Luke I, 54), he apparently considers " Israel " the subject:

> Israell has vnder law,
> hiw awne son in his awe,
> By menys of his mercy.

Towneley also gives a unique interpretation to the Vulgate reading: " Ecce enim ut facta est vox salutationis tuae in auribus meis, exultavit in gaudio infans in utero meo." This becomes:

> ffor syn that tyme full well I wote,
> The stevyn of angell voce it smote,
> And rang now in myn ere;
> A selcouth thyng is me betyde,
> The chyld makes Ioy, as any byrd,
> That I in body bere.

The second line of this quotation would seem to refer, not to Mary's greeting but to the voice of the Angel Gabriel, either when he announced the mystery of the incarnation to Mary, or at some other time known only to the playwright. Of course this may be just another case of bad translation. We must take note, however, that no amount of juggling between Latin and English has impaired or even affected the true rôle of Mary as she is pictured in the authentic Gospel narrative.

[43] *Op. cit.*, p. 39.   [44] *Op. cit.*, pp. 74-75.

THE TRIAL OF JOSEPH AND MARY

Here again we have a play which involves the miraculous incarnation of Christ in Mary. *Joseph's Return* is a coarse play, but the *Trial of Joseph and Mary* is coarser still. The development of this play is more painful than fascinating. When it terminates quite as we should desire, even then we are more gratified that the end is come than joyful at the triumph of Joseph and Mary.

Two disgusting scandalmongers,[45] aware of Mary's pregnancy, after exchanging on the stage their by no means edifying opinion of the betrothed, take care to waft their discovery to the ears of *Episcopus*. Just what connection, if any, these two evil messengers may have in the evolving of the Moralities from the Mystery Plays I cannot determine, nor have I seen the matter anywhere discussed. At any rate, *Raiseslander* and *Backbiter,* as the zealous pair are called, suggest the impersonation of abstractions that characterizes the Moralities.[46] *Episcopus* lays the burden of blame upon Joseph and immediately (though he is grieved to do so) summons the two before him. Joseph is first made to drink the potion [47] which, if it affect him for ill, will prove his guilt. He willingly performs all of the prescribed ritual,[48] is totally unharmed and receives the joyful acquittal of the Bishop. Since suspicion now naturally points entirely to Mary, she too is most willing to undergo the trial and is gloriously vindicated before all. *Primus detractor,* enraged at this turn of events, alleges that the potion was tampered with in some way by order of *Episcopus* and its harmful effects removed, because Mary was of kin to the Bishop. *Episcopus* in his turn orders the accuser to drink of the potion himself before all

[45] The story of the play is found in *Protevang.* XV-XVI, and *Pseudo-Matthew,* XII.

[46] Pollard believes that this tendency toward the personification of abstract ideas, a mark of late date in the history of the Miracle play, helps to link the Coventry cycle to the earlier Moralities.—*English Miracle Plays,* Intro., xxxix.

[47] This trial by ordeal seems to have been derived ultimately from the Book of Numbers, V, 11-31.

[48] This consisted of drinking the water "of God's vengeance," then walking around the altar seven times.

> Be-cawse þou demyst þat we do falshede.

Primus detractor no sooner swallows a draught of the stuff when he exclaims:

> Out out Alas what heylith my sculle
> A myn heed with ffyre me thynkyth is brent
> Mercy good mary I do me repent
> Of my cursyd and ffals langage.

And Mary immediately answers:

> Now god lord in hevyn omnypotent
> of his gret mercy ȝour seknes aswage.

Poor Joseph as usual receives the severest maltreatment. Mary is spared as much as the story will allow. Everyone condemns "that old shrewe Joseph." When *Episcopus* learns of the detractors' tale he would immediately exonerate Mary:

> Herke ȝe felaways why speke ȝe such schame
> Of þat good virgyn ffayr mayd mary
> ȝe be a-cursyd so hire for to defame
> Sche þat is of lyff so good and holy
> Of hire to speke suche velany
> ȝe make myn hert ful hevy of mood
> I charge ȝow sese of ȝoure fals cry
> Ffor she is sybbe of myn owyn blood.
>
> Take good heed serys what ȝe doth say
> A-vyse ȝow wele what ȝe present
> ȝyf þis be fownd fals a-nothyr day
> Ful sore ȝe xal ȝour tale repent.
>
> This evy talys my hert doth greve
> of hire to here such fowle dalyawnce

Mary's words, as usual, are redolent of the purest piety. She repeats over and over again her total guiltlessness.

> Of god in hevyn I take wyttnes
> þat synful werk was nevyr my thought
> I am a mayd ȝit of pure clennes
> lyke as I was in to þis werd brought.[49]

---

[49] This line seems suggestive of the contemporary controversy regarding Mary's conception: Was she really conceived immaculate, or, like John the Baptist, merely born without sin? Cf. Holweck, "The Immaculate Conception of the B. V. M.," in *Catholic Encyclopedia*, VII (1913), 674-680.

3

My name I hope is saff and sownde
god to wyttnes I am a mayd
Of ffleschly lust and gostly wownde
In dede nere thought I nevyr a-sayd.
I trostyn in his grace I xal hym nevyr greve
his servaunt I am in worde dede and thought

I think it is significant that the author seems to place Mary entirely in a position of self-defense. She repeatedly asserts her own innocence but seems aloof from the trouble of her spouse. This is simply another indication that the whole play is woven about Mary's vindication. Of course Joseph is bound to receive here, as elsewhere, his usual quota of mistreatment; but the whole piece has a climactic structure which clearly points to the author's intent to make the play a glorious testimony to the virginity of the Mother of God. Mary's words in one instance nicely illustrate this:

O gracyous god as þou hast chose me
ffor to be þi modyr of me to be born
saue þi tabernacle þat clene is kepte for þe
which now am put at repref and skorn
Gabryel me tolde with wordys he be-forn
þat ȝe of ȝour goodnes wold be-come my chylde
help now of ȝour hyȝness my wurchep be not lorn
A dere sone I pray ȝow help ȝour modyr mylde.

At this point the real climax of the play is reached. Mary's purgation is complete, her vindication is secure, she has proved that at once she is both mother and maid. *Episcopus,* forced by strict logic to admit it, testifies to her great prerogative:

Almyghty god what may þis mene
Ffor alle þe drynke of goddys potacyon
þis woman with chylde is fayr and clene
with-owtyn fowle spotte or maculacion
I can nat be non ymagynacion
Preve hyre gylty and synful of lyff
it sheweth opynly by here purgacion
Sche is clene mayde bothe modyr and wyff.

Another indication that the apocryphal story is pointedly made a tribute to Mary, not merely as vindicated Virgin, but primarily as Mother of God, is seen in the fact that *Episcopus* clearly senses this honor in her without once having been told about it:

We alle on knes ffall here on grownd
þou goddys hande-mayd prayng for grace
all cursyd langage and schame on sownd
good mary ffor-ȝeve us here in þis place.
Now blyssyd virgyne we thank ȝow alle
of ȝoure good hert and gret pacyens
we wyl go with ȝow hom to ȝour halle
to do ȝow servys with hyȝ reverens . . .
Than ffare wel mayden and pure virgyne
ffare wel trewe hand-mayd of god in blys
we all to ȝow lowly inclyne
and take oure leve of ȝow as wurthy is.

All things considered, the play as a whole, coarse as it is, is a tribute to the Virgin Mother of Christ. Although the *Trial* is not a part of the Virgin Group of Coventry, Mary is dramatized with the same Christological reverence that she receives in those plays. The *Trial of Joseph* is the last of the distinctly Marian plays in the Coventry cycle.

Gayley, speaking of Mary in the plays in which she is triumphant under various trying circumstances, conveys the idea that her rôle is closely allied with romance, with the " conquering heroine " type, and that, with Joseph she appeals to sentiments of sexual chivalry and admiration; also that she figures in the development of early romantic comedy.[50] I hope I have shown that her rôle is entirely too religious to lend itself to that form of romance which exploits any of the more human dramatic utilities such as sexual chivalry, jealousy, etc. Nowhere in these plays is Mary's rôle drawn out of the Christocentric halo.

[50] *Plays of Our Forefathers*, London, 1908, pp. 195-198.

CHAPTER III

I have conveniently grouped into a separate section the plays treating of Christ's Birth, the *Shepherd* and *Magi* plays, the *Purification, Flight into Egypt* and *Christ with the Doctors*. We shall find that a great deal of the dramatic focus passes from Mary to Christ, and that the former is scarcely ever presented apart from her Son. There is a surprising amount of worshipful tenderness contained in this group of plays, a tenderness that reflects strongly on the simple piety of the period. The shepherds adore Christ with tender tribute, offering their homely gifts, and uttering praises to the Child and the Mother. Mary bids the herdsmen go forth and spread the glad tidings—a rubric which accords in some measure with St. Luke's narrative, II, 18: " And all that heard, wondered; and at those things that were told them by the shepherds."

It is noteworthy that York's account of the Nativity introduces a reference gathered from a misreading of Habacuc, III, 2, in the Alexandrine version, and quoted in *Pseudo-Matt.*, 13, as " in medio animalium," instead of " in medio annorum ":

Joseph:

> O! nowe is fulfilled, for-suth I see,
> þat Abacuc in mynde gon mene
>   and preched by prophicie,—
> He saide oure sauyoure shall be sene
>   betwene bestis lye;
> And now I see þe same in sight.

The misreading is also quoted in the Augustinian *Sermo contra Judaeos*. The ox and the ass became known as the animals referred to, because of Isaias' text, I, 3, " The ox doth know his owner, and the ass his master's crib." [1] Even the Roman missal has adopted the same idea: " In medio duorum animalium innotesceris . . ." (*Tractus* for Good Friday's Mass of the Catechumens).

---

[1] Cf. Hemingway, *English Nativity Plays*, p. 272.

62

THE BIRTH OF CHRIST

The first play under study in this section, the *Birth of Christ*, bears a theme that allows wide scope for portraying the Virgin in her character of mother. The dramatists have succeeded in doing this, and the Virgin they picture is the familiar Virgin of the stable scene at Bethlehem, the Virgin of the crèche—adoring, solicitous for the Infant Saviour's every want. Joseph's rôle, while not handled altogether disrespectfully, lacks the consistent reverence attaching to Mary's part. Of the three cycles, Towneley alone omits the story of the Nativity. The rest give it ample treatment. Coventry, as usual, is on hand with a few homely touches. Thus, Joseph grumbles with all the impatience of the annoyed husband when he learns that all men are to go into their own city for enrollment. Mary accepts the decree more optimistically:

> Myn husbond and my spowse with 3ow wyl I wende
> A syght of þat cyte ffayn wolde I se
> If I myght of myn Alye ony þer ffynde
> It wolde be grett joye on to me.

The utterance of Mary seems an idle insertion on the part of the author, or at least something irrelevant to what we might expect of the woman shortly to give birth to the Saviour. Was it not that the playwright wanted more than anything else to stress the fact that Mary was of the family of David, and skillfully makes her allude to her relatives in the city of Bethlehem—David's city? We discover similar precautions a few lines above this in the text, when Joseph also is made to announce his Davidic descent:

> I þat am a pore tymbre wryth borne of þe blood of dauyd
> þe Emperorys comawndement I must holde with
> And ellys I were to blame.

In the journey to Bethlehem, Coventry introduces the cherry tree episode,[1a] wherein Mary, espying a cherry tree in full blossom, bids Joseph pluck her a bit of its fruit. After a vain and reluctant effort, finding the tree too high, he drops the indelicate remark:

> · . . . lete hym pluk 3ow cheryes be-gatt 3ow with childe.

[1a] A fairly detailed account of this legend, especially in its medieval circulation in ballad form, is given by Vriend, *op. cit.*, pp. 105-110.

Mary prays accordingly:

> Now good lord I pray þe graunt me þis boun
> to haue of þese cheries and it be ʒour wylle

and immediately the tree stoops to her while she picks the fruit to her heart's content.   Joseph, ashamed and deeply penitent, exclaims:

> Ow I know weyl I haue offendyd my god in trinyte
> Spekyng to my spowse these vnkynde wurdys
> Ffor now I beleve wel it may non other be
> but þat my spowse berygth þe kyngys son of blys
> He help us now at oure nede
> of þe kyndrede of jesse worthely were ʒe bore
> Kyngys and patryarkys ʒow be-ffore
> all þese wurthy of ʒour kyndred wore
> as clerkys in story rede.

Miss Swenson [2] seems slightly disconcerted at finding that this episode is written in the tumbling meter, whereas the rest of the play is in simple double quatrains.[3] However, I can see no objection to crediting the piece to the original playwright.   In the first place, the episode in tone is not alien to the context of the play, for the play as a whole, as I shall shortly indicate, besides testifying to the birth of the God-Man, heavily emphasizes the divine maternity of Mary, and, of course, its concomitant prerogative, her spotless virginity.   Now, the sullenness of Joseph in the cherry tree story, and above all, his indelicate remark, are simply foils whereby to add vividness to his splendid confession of Mary's purity and the divinity of the Child in her womb. Nothing could have better suited the dramatist.   Moreover, note that the scene is introduced in the journey to Bethlehem, whereas *Pseudo-Matthew,* its source, together with the other works mentioned by Vriend, connect it with the Flight into Egypt.   This fact points unerringly to the purposefulness of the author in

---

[2] *Op. cit.,* p. 33.

[3] Throughout the medieval period there is evidence enough that such a change in meter was consistently used to accentuate the humor of broad scenes.   For a full discussion of this matter, see p. lxv and ff. of the introduction to Robert Lee Ramsay's edition of *Magnyfycence,* EETS. ES. xcviii. See also " Changes in Verse-Technic in the Sixteenth Century English Drama," by Gildersleeve in *American Journal of Philology,* No. 31, p. 180 (1910).

inserting it here; his obvious and only purpose is to stress the
divine maternity and the virginity of Mary. Regarding the
meter, I think it plausible to say that the dramatist deliberately
chose to effect a facetious turn by applying the principle of metri-
cal contrast. In the Moralities, for instance, it became a commonplace to indicate absence of dignity in a character by giving the
verse less majesty of movement. In addition, do not the last four
lines of Joseph's confession seem put there designedly to reinforce
the fact, stated indirectly at the beginning of the play, that Mary
is of Davidic descent?

Although these facts as a whole testify to the Christocentric
portrayal of Mary in the Coventry play, still I think the following
excerpts offer a too valuable brand of evidence to go unheeded;
the evidence, I mean, stressing the divine maternity and the
virgin birth.

Maria (upon reaching their wretched lodging):

> In þis pore logge my chawmere I take
> here for to A-byde þe blyssyd byrth
> of hym þat all this werd dude make
> be-twyn myn sydys I fele he styrth . . .
> Joseph myn husbond a-bydyn here I xal
> ffor here wyl be born þe Kyngys sone of blys.

Joseph laments the impoverished reception-place that must be
accorded the Son of God:

> god be þin help spowse it swemyth me sore
> þus febyly loggyd and in so pore degre
> goddys sone amonge bestys to be bore
> his woundyr werkys ffulfyllyd must be.

The remainder of the Coventry *Nativity* is given over to the story
of the midwives, which will later be treated conjointly with the
· same story in Chester. Meanwhile let us briefly review the Marian
element in the story of the birth of Christ as contained in this
last cycle.

As in Coventry, Joseph groans at the inconvenience of having
to travel to Bethlehem. He consoles himself, however, with the
significant thought:

> The angel to me tolde:
> he that shold man out of bale bring
> my wief had in her kepinge,
> that semes all good to my liking
> And makes me more bold.

On the way to Bethlehem the story is introduced in which Mary beholds a vision of two groups of people, the one exulting, the other weeping. The vision is explained by an angel as a "token" of the joy and the sorrow that the approaching birth of Christ is to bring upon men according as they shall believe in Him or not.[4] The wording of this incident clearly indicates the dramatist's diligence in rendering to Mary the full status rightfully hers. And yet, while bestowing various beautiful titles upon her, such as "God's mother deare" and "the treasure of heaven," he is careful to have us keep in mind that only in virtue of the Child in her womb do these honors belong to her, only because of "Abraham's seede."

We now come to the scene of the midwives, contained in the two cycles. It is studied from many angles by Vriend;[5] here, however, I must restrict myself merely to its bearing on the rôle of Mary. Like the cherry tree episode, it is ultimately a climactic testimony to the divinity of Christ and the virginity of Mary. While Joseph is seeking the two women, Mary gives birth to Jesus. In Chester, as he returns with the midwives, she joyfully exclaims:

> A! Ioseph, tydinges aright:
> I haue a sonne, a sweet wight.
> lord, thanked be thou, much of mighte,
> for preeved is thy postye!
> penance non I felt this night
> but right so as he in me light,
> comen is he here in my sight,
> Gods sonne, as you may see.

I would call attention to this last stanza, inasmuch as Coventry is equally insistent upon the painlessness of Mary's deliverance.

---

[4] Based on *Protevang.*, XVII, *Pseudo-Matthew*, XIII, and also contained in the *Golden Legend* (Cap. VI; ed. Graesse, p. 41), and in the *Stanzaic Life of Christ*, ed. Foster, EETS. OS. 166 (1926), 12 ff.

[5] *Op. cit.*, pp. 97-101.

Each cycle evidently thereby seeks to stress the supernatural character of the whole event:

> Of þis fayr byrth þat here is myn
> Peyne nere grevynge fele I ryght non
> I am clene mayde and pure virgyn

This very last line indicates the theme for which the scene of the midwives is apparently solely introduced—the virgin birth, and, of course in consequence, the divinity of the Child. In both plays the scene winds up with the midwives paying a prolonged tribute to the " mayde " and to her " gloryous Chylde and kynge of blysse." Of the two midwives one is incredulous of the virgin birth, and, seeking to verify things is stricken with palsy. In each play *Angelus* bids the incredulous one adore the Child if she will have forgiveness and cure. And, important to note, in each play she combines this adoration with sentiments of worship of Mary; in other words, the juxtaposition of Mother and Child recurs, and serves to finish the Nativity story with a grand flourish, as it were, of tribute to Mary and Jesus, to the virginity of the one and the divinity of the Other — a thoroughly Christocentric situation, highly suggestive of the fervid devotion of St. Bernard. Thus, in Chester, the penitent midwife prays:

> Ah! sweet childe, I aske mercye
> for thy mothers love, marye,
> though I haue wroughte wretchedlye:
> sweet childe, forgeve yt mee!

And in Coventry:

> O gloryous chylde and kynge of blysse
> I aske ȝow mercy for my trespace
> I knowledge my synne I demyd a-mys
> O blyssyd babe grawnt me sum grace
> Of ȝow mayde Also here in þis place
> I aske mercy knelynge on kne
> most holy mayde grawnt me solace
> Sum wurde of comforte sey now to me.

Coventry rounds out the play a little more than Chester, protracting the praises of the Divine Child and the Virgin Mother. The following lines sound and re-sound the dominant note of the entire play in each cycle:

Maria: As goddys Aungel to ȝow dede telle
             my chyld is medycyn ffor every sor
Salome: A now blyssyd be þis chylde euer more
             þe son of god for sothe he is . . .
             In every place I xal telle þis
             Of a clene mayd þat god is born
             And in oure lyknes god now clad is
             Mankend to saue þat was for-lorn
             His modyr a mayde as sche was be-forn
             natt fowle polutyd as other women be
             but fayr and fresch as rose on thorn
             Lely wyte clene with pure virginyte.

The constant insistence in both cycles upon the bodily integrity of Mary finds a parallel in the following lines from a thirteenth century hymn to the Virgin:

> Swetelic ure louerd hit diȝte
> þat þu maide wiþ-ute were.
> þat al þis world bicluppe ne miȝte
> þu sscholdest of þin boseme bere.
> þe ne stiȝte ne þe ne priȝte.
> in side. in lende. ne elles where.
> þat wes wiþ ful muchel riȝte:
> for þu bere þine helere.[6]

York's treatment of the birth of Christ is hardly more than an enlargement of St. Luke's narrative. The play begins with a short enactment of Joseph's seeking shelter for his spouse with child, since the town is crowded. While he is out seeking fuel for their miserable shed, the Child is born. The lines of both Mary and Joseph, especially in adoring the Infant, need not be quoted here, since it suffices to note that the divinity of the Child is repeatedly hailed in the tenderest terms. The scene ends with the holy couple pledging themselves to the eternal service of the divine Infant. Mary's virginity is not alluded to, all the emphasis going to her motherhood. She is here most dramatically portrayed as Mother of God. The extended stable scene throws this prerogative

---

[6] *Old English Homilies*, II, ed. Morris, EETS. OS. 53 (1872), Appendix, p. 257.

into bold relief, while primarily focusing the birth of the God-Man.[7]

THE ADORATION OF THE SHEPHERDS

The Shepherds plays, together with the story of the Magi, cannot now offer us very much material for treatment, since most of the Marian element has been extracted and dealt with under the heading, *Other Mariological Prophetae.* Each cycle, however, contains enough remaining material to illustrate conclusively the Christocentricity of the Virgin's rôle.

In Coventry, Moses and Daniel are the only prophets cited who allude to Mary. Aside from this indirect quotation, all the discussion among the shepherds centers upon the Christ Child. The same is the case in York, whose only shepherd-play prophets involving Mary are Isaias and Balaam. Chester's shepherds likewise confine their discussion—in the midst of their sport—to the Christ Child; and Towneley I, while citing Moses and Isaias in reference to Our Lady, allows its herdsmen to discuss in scholarly fashion the other prophecies relative to the coming of Christ.[8] In all four cases we find that the focal point in the minds of the shepherds is the new born Saviour. The interesting and climactic scene of each play is that wherein the humble herdsmen adore the Child. In Coventry, Towneley and York they fill out this scene with lyrically adoring the Child, without at all addressing themselves to Mary. In Towneley I, II, and in Coventry, Mary blesses them and promises to pray to her Child for them, by way of gratitude. Chester, however, seizes the opportunity to have Mary inform the shepherds of her Child's divinity and of her own virginity:

[7] York makes distinct mention of the crib:

Here in þis cribbe I myght þe lay.

(Y. p. 116, line 118)

Chambers (*Medieval Stage*, II, 42-43) discusses the history of the crib, or crèche. According to him St. Francis did not invent the crèche at Greccio in 1223, for it existed many centuries before St. Francis. Doubtless, however, it did not reach its widespread popularity until after St. Francis constructed his in Italy. The protracted stable scene of York would seem to indicate that the crèche tradition influenced this cycle more than the others.

[8] These other prophets in the shepherd plays are tabulated by Miss Swenson, *op. cit.*, pp. 24-25.

> Shepheardes, sothlie I see,
> that my sonne you hither sent
> through Gods might in maiesty,
> that in me light, and here is lent.

She goes on to explain that she was married to Joseph by divine ordinance only, as she says, " but to keepe my virginity." Joseph corroborates her words, stressing that another main purpose was the avoidance of slander. He concludes:

> therfore goes! prech forth this thinge,
> all together and not in twyn,
> that you have seene your heavenlie King
> comen all mankind to wyn.

York seems to give no part at all to Mary; still it is beyond doubt that she must have appeared in the play, either holding the Child or watching over Him in the cold night.[9]

Towneley II, aside from the single indirect quotation from Isaias, supplies its shepherds with lines anticipatory of their meeting with both Mother and Child:

Primus pastor: hy we theder for thy;
> If we be wete and wery,
> To that chyld and that lady
> we haue it not to lose.

And upon entering the stable the same *pastor* exclaims:

> hayll, comly and clene! hayll, yong child!
> hayll, maker, as I meyne, of a madyn so mylde!

All of these shepherd scenes are apparently little more than the Gospel story amplified—omitting, of course, the interesting non-canonical matter as presented by the Towneley and Chester shepherds, particularly the famous Mak episode. As far as the adoration scenes are concerned, however, the matter is purely Christocentric. Doubtless it was hard for the dramatists to find anything to say for Mary, especially inasmuch as the Gospel records nothing. But rather than impose anything non-Christocentric upon her, they keep her in comparative silence. Chester was able to extend

---

[9] Compare T., p. 140, lines 746-747:

Primus pastor: Ffarewell, lady, so fare to beholde,
> With thy childe on thi kne.

her part a little more than the other cycles, and her very words
indicate that she is depicted only as the Virgin Mother. It is
noteworthy that the Chester dramatist, while handling Mary's
rôle so reverently, nevertheless takes liberties with Joseph —
although the Scripture story is silent upon him at this point:

Primus Pastor (upon entering the stable) :
what ever this olde man, that heare is,
take heede howe his head is hore,
his beard like a buske of breeres
with a pownd of heare about his mouth and more.

Tertius Pastor:
why! with his beard though it be rough,
right well to her he heedes;
worthy wight, wit wold we now:
will ye warne us, worthy in weedes?

We observe then, that although, as in Towneley and Chester,
the shepherds make a revel of their watching, the atmosphere
changes in the adoration scene, which, in all the plays, is deeply
religious and reverent. The few words that we have from Mary
in these scenes indicate strongly that her rôle as Mother of God
has not altered, and that the requisite veneration becoming her
is still present—expressed in Towneley II, and implicit in other
plays.

THE ADORATION OF THE MAGI

The Magi plays of course, follow close (chronologically) upon
the Shepherds plays. Both treat Mary in quite the same manner.
Considerable attention is given the story of the Magi in each cycle.
In general there is no departure from the story as we know it—the
journey of the kings, their meeting with Herod, the latter's plot
to destroy the new born Child, and the presentation of gifts, gold,
frankincense, and myrrh.[10] Chester is a little more elaborate in
depicting the jealous Herod's consternation and his frantic search
after prophecies concerning this new King. Here, unlike the
Shepherd plays in general, we are presented with matter touching
upon the Virgin before the adoration scene takes place. Every line
breathes reverence for her as the Mother of Christ. Thus, in

[10] Kretzmann finds striking liturgical tags in these plays. *Op. cit.*, pp.
64-65.

Chester, *Angelus* addresses the kings:

> the chylde you seche, there shall you see,
> borne all of a mayden free,
> that kinge of heauen and earth shall be,
> and all mankind forbye.

Tertius Rex, nearing the stable, exclaims:

> A fayre mayden, Sirres, yonder I see,
> an olde man sittinge at her knee,
> a childe also, as thinkes me,
> three persons ther-in arne.

This theme of Mother and Son seems to characterize all the Magi plays. Continuing in Chester, Mary thanks the kings, adding:

> And leaves, Lordes, without were,
> that to my sonne you shall be dere,
> that hym to-day hath honoured here
> and me also for his sake.

Joseph in the same play is careful to insist upon the virginity of his spouse, telling the Magi:

> keper of her virginitie
> I haue ben many a day.

He further advises:

> Therfore I wot forsooth, I-wis,
> cleane mayden that she is
> and with man did never amisse,
> and therof be you bolde.

> But of the Holy Ghost this is,
> for to bringe mankinde to blisse,
> and this chylde is very his,
> so Gabriel me toulde.

In York, where the Magi stand at the threshold of the Child's dwelling place, *Secundus Rex* answers to inquiry thus:

> We seke a barne þat all shall bylde,
> His sartayne syngne hath saide vs soo,
> And his modir, a mayden mylde,
> Her hope we to fyne þam twoo.

When *Tertius Rex* in the same play is offering his gift of myrrh, he includes in his eloquent prayer the significant lines:

> Hayll! man þat is made to þi men meete,
> Sen þou and thy modir with mirthis ar mette.

Mary's words of gratitude take the form chiefly of an assurance
that their journey has not been in vain, that all is true that they
had hoped to find. The author does not fail to use this opportunity for a brief rehearsal of the incarnation. Mary continues:

> For I consayued my sonne sartayne
> With-outen misse of man in mynde,
> And bare hym here with-outen payne,
> Where women are wonte to be pynyd.
> Goddis aungell in his gretyng playne,
> Saide he shulde comforte al man kynde,
> Thar-fore doute yow no dele,
> Here for to haue youre bone,
> I shall witnesse full wele,
> All þat is saide and done.

Towneley portrays Mary for us after the Magi have finished
offering their gifts. She first of all assures the kings of her Son's
limitless might. Then:

> This chyld, that on me borne has bene,
> All bayll may blyn;
> I am his moder, and madyn clene
> withoutten syn.
> Therfor, lordyngys, where so ye fare,
> Boldly looke ye tell ay whare
> how I this blyst of bosom bare,
> That best shalbe;
> And madyn cleyn, as I was are,
> Thrugh his pauste.

In Coventry, *Primus Rex* announces his mission:

> Of prophetys speche I am ware
> Therfore a ferre way I fare
> A maydenys childe to seche

Tertius Rex, describing the Child whom he is searching for, says
that He " In a maydonys flesch is clad." *Primus Rex* later reiter-
ates the theme: " He is born of a mayd ȝynge . . ." The prayer
of the same king kneeling before the Infant includes the following:

Heyle be þou kyng Cold clade
heyll with maydynnys mylk fade
heyll I cum to þe with gold glade

Tertius Rex echoes the sentiment:

Lord I knele downe be thy bede
In maydyns fleshe þou arte hede.

His prayer toward the end of the play, besides bearing upon the point in hand, is uncommonly touching and beautiful:

Broþer I must lye þe bye
I will go neuer ouer þis stye
Tyll I haue a slepe
The yong kyng and his moþer mary
Saue vs all frome euery velany
Now Cryst vs save and kepe.

This little petition has all the flavor of a Compline prayer.

In each of the cycles, it is evident that Mary's rôle in the Magi scene is nothing different from what we have previously seen it to be. The theme of Mother and Child is abundantly in evidence. Doubtless the words of the Gospel account very much for its under-lined presence in these plays: " And entering into the house, they found the Child with Mary his mother . . ." [11]

THE PURIFICATION

I have previously remarked that, if we could definitely establish a liturgical tradition in the cyclic plays, we should have little trouble in accounting for the consistent Christocentricity of the Virgin's rôle. Research work has been done in seeking a liturgical basis for the early drama in general. Kretzmann's monograph [12] is the most notable contribution. It is a well-nigh complete com-pendium of parallels between the drama and liturgy. Other stud-ies have been published on the topic, but they comprise a list too lengthy for record here. Professor George R. Coffman, in his review of Dr. Carghill's *Drama and Liturgy*, has included an extensive bibliography on the subject.[13] Although, as I have also

[11] Matt. ii. 11.
[12] *The Liturgical Element in the Earliest Forms of the Medieval Drama.*
[13] *Speculum*, VI (1931), No. 4, pp. 612-613.

remarked elsewhere, this present work lies outside the range of that much mooted question, I feel that my essay, striving, as it does, to unveil the Christocentric nature of the Virgin's rôle, will contribute, in some measure, towards proving that to a large extent the cyclic plays actually are the projections of liturgical tradition. It seems to me that a student following up the evidence that I have here gathered, and singling out parallels in contemporary writings—particularly sermons and homilies—could definitely link up the Virgin cult, as seen in the drama, with very clear-cut liturgical traditions. He would discover, I am sure, that the cyclic plays are for the most part an outgrowth of popular tradition. And from here he should have but little trouble in proving that popular tradition, when it deals with scriptural matter, and particularly when it lives in a Catholic people, can have its source only in the piety of the people; and the piety of a Catholic people lives in the liturgy. I call attention to these few facts mostly to preface what I shall show to be the deep rooted tradition upon which the playwrights were modelling their pieces in the Purification story. The nature of the Virgin's rôle in the plays will be better understood by a consideration of that background.

The feast of the Purification of Mary and Presentation of Christ in the Temple has been one of the chief English festivals of Mary almost from the introduction of Christianity into the British Isles. It also goes under the name of Candlemas-day, owing to the procession which took place, with the laity included, each person holding a lighted candle. The Abbot Aelfric tells us:

> On the mass-day that is called the Purification of Saint Mary, you shall bless candles and carry them in procession singing hymns of praise, both clerics and laymen, and offer them thus burning after the gospel to the mass-priest during the offertory-song.[14]

The character of the feast is further seen in Mirk's *De Purificacione Beate Marie et Eius Solempnitate:*

> Good Cristen men and woymen, þat louyþe to serve oure lady, and to fast hur evens bred and watyr in hegh mede to you, such a day ȝe schull

---

[14] B. Fehr, *Die Hirtenbriefe Aelfrics* (Bibliothek der Angels. prosa, Band IX) Hamburg (1914), 214. (Quoted in Vriend, p. 114.)

have Candylmasse-day; wherfor doþe in þat even as your deuocyon techeþe you. For, þat day holy Chyrch maketh gret melody yn worschyppe of hyr and of hyr swete sonne Ihesu Crist, our Lord, specyalt yn þtre þynges: yn our layd puryfiyng, in Symones metyng, and yn candels offryng.[15]

This prefatory matter will clarify my treatment of Mary's rôle in the Purification plays.

In each of the plays, save that in Towneley, Mary is the first to bring up the topic of repairing to the Temple for purification.[16] Joseph does not oppose her.[17] His answers to her, while proclaiming her purity and divine maternity, also tell us the traditional reason why Mary did not exempt herself from a law not binding her;[18] thus in Chester, Joseph says:

> yea, marye, though it be no nede,
> seith thou arte cleane in thoughte and deed,
> yet it is good to do as god bade,
> and worcke after his lawe

And in Coventry:

> To be purefyed haue ȝe no nede
> ne þi son to be offeryd so god me spede
> ffor fyrst þou art ful clene
> Vndefowlyd in thought and dede

---

[15] *Mirk's Festial*, EETS. ES. 96 (1905), 56-57.

[16] The law is to be found in Lev. xii. 6.

[17] The Coventry civic plays, however, while handling the Virgin's rôle with complete delicacy, do not miss the opportunity to bring in some ridiculous comedy at the expense of Joseph.—*Two Coventry Plays*, pp. 47-51.

[18] From the fact that none of the Purification plays is in chronological order, Kretzmann sees an indication that they are isolated outgrowths of the liturgy (p. 72). According to St. Luke's narrative (chap. 2), the *Purification* immediately follows the *Nativity*. In Towneley, however, it is situated between the *Herod* play and the play of the *Doctors*. In Coventry it follows the *Slaughter* play, likewise in Chester. And in York it occurs after the play of the *Disciples of Emmaus*, although, according to Miss Smith (p. 433), it should have been placed between the *Adoration of the Magi* and the *Flight into Egypt*. Even here, nevertheless, the play would be chronologically impossible.

In his study of the Purification plays, C. Davidson says: "The agreement among the plays is that of a common church tradition, reinforced by literary convention. This episode, together with that of Joseph and Mary's journey to the temple, bears the marks of the later literary fashion in most of the plays."—*Studies in the English Mystery Plays*, p. 164.

and a-nothyr þi son with-owtyn drede
is god and man to mene
Wherefore it nedyd not to bene
but to kepe þe lawe on moyses wyse

This strain continues in York and Towneley. Joseph alleges her exemption, but Mary, model of obedience to God's law, insists upon going to the temple. Thus in the four cycles we see allusions to the great lesson that the story of the Purification is designed to impart to Catholics: obedience to the law of God. Christians have ever regarded Mary as the model of this obedience in her purification, for whereas the law did not bind her—and the cycles are emphatic on this point—nevertheless she conformed to its prescription.[19]

We notice therefore the reverence with which the Virgin-rôle is here dealt with thus far. She is not exploited dramatically. Her dignity revolves about Christ, and there is an atmosphere of piety, even of didacticism, surrounding her appearance as far as we have studied it. The plays continue much in the Gospel fashion. In Coventry the scene is brief, with no essential departure from St. Luke's narrative. It is the same in the other three cycles, with the exception that Simeon is more minutely delineated and his decrepitude described.[20] In Towneley the bells of the temple start ringing of themselves as the holy trio approach, and two angels are employed to announce the good tidings to Simeon.[21] York's

[19] Cf. *Old English Homilies*, ed. by Morris, EETS. ES. 53 (1892), 46: " Such a rite Purification was observed in those days; and Our Lady Saint Mary, the heavenly queen, observed it in childbed, in offering and in churching, and we ought to follow her good example . . ."

In *Mirk's Festial*, pp. 56-57, Mary is described as having conformed to a legality not binding her, first, to obey Scripture, which bids men to be meeker even as they grow greater; second, to show respect for the law; third, to " stop mouths " that might otherwise see scandal; and fourth, to give good example to Christian women.

[20] See Taylor, " The Relation of the English Corpus Christi Play to the Middle English Religious Lyric," *Modern Philology*, V (1907).

[21] The Digby *Purification* elaborates this point of the story most roundly. Virgins are to come forth, with lighted tapers, to

worship this Child, very God and man,
Offrid in this temple be his moder dere.

There is also an elaborate candle procession in Digby. See *The Digby Plays*, ed. by Furnivall, EETS. ES. 70 (1896), 19-20.

account is prefaced by a long prologue in which *Prisbeter* descants upon the fact that God created all men and bade them keep His laws. Chester offers a few deviations. The first is that in which Simeon, taking up the book of Isaias to read about the advent of Christ, comes upon the *concipiet* prophecy. He begins to doubt the feasibility of a virgin conceiving; so, erasing the word " virgin," he substitutes " good woman " in its stead. Replacing the book and entering into a conversation with Anna, the prophetess, about the coming of the Messiah, he again has occasion to refer to the book, but to his amazement finds the word " virgin " restored in brilliant red letters. Again he scratches it out but shortly after finds it restored in letters of gold. There seems to be no definite source for this peculiar legend. Miss Foster has a discussion upon the question in her introduction to the *Stanzaic Life*,[22] but nothing final is arrived at. The other point of special interest in Chester is the fact that Joseph offers a waxen candle,[23] and signalizes it as a symbol of Mary's virginity:

Joseph: A signe I offer here also
              of virgine waxe, as other moe,
              in tockeninge shee has lived oo
              in full devocion.
              and sir semion, leve well this:
              as cleane as this waxe nowe is,
              as cleane is my wife, I-wisse,
              from all corruptcion.

Mary's rôle here is consistently Christocentric. Throughout these Purification plays she is portrayed only as the pure Mother of the Saviour. In fact, the juxtaposition of Mother and Son seems the dominant theme.[24] Thus, in Towneley:

[22] P. xxvii.

[23] This is reminiscent of an old church custom, dating back from Anglo-Saxon times, in which the faithful presented to the church the candles carried at procession, that they might be of use during the year. See Liebermann, F., *Gesetze der Angelsachsen*, Niemeyer, 1903-1916, VIII Aethelred 12, 1; Cnut 12.

[24] Even despite the lengthy part given to Simeon. His rôle, extended as it is, adapts itself to the play only in its connection with the climactic scene of the offering of the Child. Otherwise he is only incidental to the central story, for he merely recounts his feebleness, etc. Doubtless the playwrights considered his long monologues an excellent introduction, or prologue.

Primus angelus (addressing Simeon) :

> Oft has thou prayd to haue a sight
> Of hym that in a madyn light;

Ioseph :

> Mary, it begynnys to pas,
> ffourty dayes syn that thou was
> Delyuer of thy son; . . .
> Therfor, mary, madyn heynd,
> Take thi chyld and let vs weynd
> The tempyll vntyll . . .

Similarly in the other three cycles, the conversation of Joseph, Simeon, Anna, *Angelus* and *Prisbeter* centers around the " babb, borne of a madyns wombe vnfylde."

York and Chester are the only cycles that allude to Simeon's utterance to Mary : " Behold this child is set for the fall, and for the resurrection of many in Israel, and for a sign which shall be contradicted; and thy own soul a sword shall pierce, that out of many hearts, thoughts may be revealed." [25] Possibly the Coventry and Towneley playwrights chose to exclude anything that might cast a shade over an otherwise thoroughly joyous affair. The latter cycle, however, is lacking the last two leaves of the *Purification* MS,[26] which may have included a reference to the Simeon utterance. It is quite possible that it may have found its way into the York and Chester plays at a later date, influenced, no doubt, by the popularity of the *Planctus* lyrics. These we shall study later on. The " sword " piercing Mary's soul is interpreted in both cycles as a reference to the Virgin's sorrows during her Son's Passion. This is the traditional interpretation among Catholics. The Fathers, with a few exceptions,[27] agreed upon it, while in the Middle Ages the idea had taken root.[28]

In summing up, then, this study of the cyclic Purification plays, we may say that Mary's rôle is handled in a thoroughly Christo-

---

[25] St. Luke ii. 34. 35.

[26] The Towneley Plays, ed. by Pollard, EETS. ES. 71 (1897), 185.

[27] St. Basil and Origen, among other Greek Fathers, misinterpret this " sword " as an allusion to a future sin of doubt in Mary. See Migne, *P. G.* 32, p. 966; 13, p. 1819 *passim*.

[28] As early as the tenth century in England, we find Aelfric alluding to the " sword " as an indication of Mary's grief at the Passion of Christ. See T. Bridgett, *Our Lady's Dowry*, p. 90.

centric fashion. There is not the slightest effort made to extend her rôle out of its definite setting. Dramatic liberties are taken with Simeon; Anna and Joseph are elaborated upon; angels are brought in, and as in Chester, a legend is introduced. But Mary is handled with the customary reverence and reticence. The words allowed her are cautiously—almost painfully—limited to what is consistent with her character. She serves no dramatic interest. She is juxtaposed, in all the plays, with her Infant Son, who is always alluded to in terms of divinity. And last, the manifest adherence to liturgical tradition enhances the Christocentricity of her rôle.

THE FLIGHT INTO EGYPT

The Gospel account of this incident is decidedly brief and clear-cut.[29] It naturally lends itself but little to dramatic expansion, and in Coventry and Chester receives only a hasty reference, being almost completely absorbed into the story of the massacre. Coventry merely employs an angel to warn Joseph, who in turn warns Mary, and the play rushes on with the slaughter scene. Chester elaborates slightly more, but with no essential change. In both plays Joseph and Mary are cheerfully docile to the angel's bidding. Towneley and York, however, have woven a fairly interesting play around such scanty Gospel material, everybody recognizing the embroidery to be apocryphal; for it is a commonplace in dealing with these plays that where one finds an expansion of the theme of the Gospel, one realizes it has its basis ultimately in the apocrypha and tradition.

In Towneley, we find a very harsh and disgruntled Joseph. At the warning of *Angelus* he bitterly complains that he is old and weary and knows not the way into Egypt. Even after *Angelus* tries to hearten him by saying,

> Ther of haue thou no drede;
> weynd furth, & leyf thi dyn;
> The way he shall you lede,
> the kyng of all man-kyn,

Joseph remains disconsolate. He sinks into another slough of despond, when Mary suddenly appears on the scene. He breaks the

[29] Matt. ii. 13. 14.

news to her, describing the blood-thirsty intention of Herod. Mary's utterance is charged with motherly instinct, but mellowed with the dignity and reverence belonging to her character of Mother of God:

> My son? alas, for care!
> who may my doyllys dyll?
> wo worth fals herode are!
> my son why shuld he spyll?
> Alas! I lurk and dare!
> To slo this barne I bare,
> what wight in warld had wyll?
> his hart shuld be full sare
> Sichon for to fare,
> That neuer yit dyd yll,
> Ne thoght.

It is worthy of notice, I think, that, however emotional this passage might seem, it nevertheless contains nothing inconsistent with the Christocentric aspect of the Virgin. We see here a touching outpouring of genuine emotion, aroused by what must naturally stir the heart of any mother—the threatening of her Child's life. Very conceivably this is another instance of where the widespread movement of devotional tenderness influenced the Mystery Plays. However, we need not linger on that point. Rather, let us look into Mary's reaction as recorded in the above quotation. The emotion, quite as we should psychologically expect (and quite to the credit of the author's insight into human conduct), assumes three forms:

a) My Son has done nothing to merit murder;

b) Alas! I am nervous and excited!

c) Herod ought to have shame in his heart for threatening the life of my innocent Son.

The three forms, be it noted, do not suggest anything compromising to the dignity and reverence belonging to Mary's Christocentricity. If Mary were to be made a secular figure, a mere woman in distress and fear, harassed by conflicts within and without, there is no doubt that here the author had a good opportunity. Although he does give play to the tenderest maternal emotions, he does so without doing violence to Mary's Christocentric rôle.

The strain continues after the last quotation given above:

Maria: Alas! how shuld I lete?
             My son that is so swete
             Is soght for to be slayn

and   his ded wold I not se,
             ffor all this warld to wyn;
             Alas! full wo were me,
             In two if we shuld twyn;
             My chyld so bright of ble,
             To slo hym were pyte,
             And a full hedus syn . . .

She is apprehensive of the journey, and calls upon God to aid them:

             Greatt god, as he well may,
             That shope both nyght and day,
             ffrom wandreth he vs were,
             And shame;
             My chyld how shuld I bere
             So far from hame? . . .
             Alas, full wo is me!
             Is none so wyll as I!
             My hart wold breke in thre,
             My son to se hym dy.

But nothing human is worked up at the expense of her super-natural character. This indicates a manifest mindfulness of the Virgin's Christocentric nature on the part of the playwright; it indicates a conscious reticence. There is not in these passages the slightest tinge of resentment or of revenge. It is the only element lacking to perfect the reaction most natural to the mother of a baby threatened to be murdered. That the motif of revenge is utilized in other connections in Towneley is apparent if only we look to the slaughter scene a little further on. Each *mulier,* to an exaggerated degree, breathes out hot vengeance on the soldier when he threatens to slay her child—curiously enough, more preoccupied with tearing out the scalp of *miles* than with pleading for the infant's life or bewailing its certain death. With Mary, however, there is no sentiment of vengeance. Such an element is too inconsistent with the character of her rôle. In the second place, Mary's great preoccupation in her moment of trouble is the welfare and the surpassing innocence of her Babe. We have here an emotionalized picture of the Mother of God protecting her Child.

Thus does the dramatist picture to us the young Mother who completely identifies herself with every concern of her Child. These lines illustrate thoroughly the Virgin in her strict rôle of Mother of God. The human element is admitted, but only to enhance the divine; for, as we have seen, the innocence and dignity of the Child is not lost sight of in the Mother's transports; in fact, it is the very stimulus of her emotion. Naturally enough, the Child Himself could take no more part in the play than to appear. But the play-wright has made it clear enough, in Mary's wording, that the Child is the central theme of the piece. In short, then, the Virgin's rôle here, clothed as it is in human sentiment, is really Christo-centric.

But another consideration will also illustrate that there is no dramatization of Mary beyond the limits of her Christocentric rôle. To begin with, the subject, by its very brevity, requires a certain amount of straining in order to be pulled into an accept-able play. We have seen that Mary's rôle has not essentially changed its true character; the author went so far and no further; a perceptible restraint marks his treatment of her. But does he exhibit that restraint with Joseph? By no means. He gives full play to pen and touches up the spouse of Mary in a fashion that must have given keen delight to the spectators. For Joseph, as I said in the beginning, grumbles roundly at the prospects of a forced retreat into Egypt, even though an angel from Heaven has an-nounced the message. And humanly enough, in his perversity, he cannot bring himself to sympathize with an alarmed mother, but must consider above all his own discomfort, going so far, in fact, as to wonder why death will not slay him and end his cares and troubles. The climax comes when he tells the groundlings that young men should beware, for marriage is making him " all wan." Toward the end of the play, however, our dramatist, quite in the face of consistency, allows a sentiment of reverence to creep in for the Gospel patriarch. For Joseph suddenly softens toward the situation and strangely seems to forget his own woes in favor of Mary.

In York, the circumstances do not alter very greatly. There is the notable difference that Joseph's attitude throughout the play is a good deal less selfish and more resigned and optimistic.[30] Mary's motherly consternation is again depicted, quite as in Towne-

---

[30] The York plays in general have a markedly reverent and biblical tone. Cf. L. Smith, *The York Plays*, Introd. xlvii. Miss Lyle, acting on the sup-

ley, so that quotations are hardly necessary here. Suffice it to say that there is introduced absolutely nothing at all in conflict with her Christocentricity. Joseph's rôle receives an added touch at the end, for, upon carrying the Child to relieve Mary, he feels his waning strength renewed.

Concluding, it is seen that Mary's rôle, while given free emotional play, loses none of its Christocentric character but rather is enhanced in that respect, for we have here an admirable picture of the devoted Mother of the divine Babe. Moreover, in a play, which, by its meager episodal proportions, calls for a large amount of dramatic strain, we find this strain relieved solely at Joseph's expense, while Mary's essential rôle is retained unimpaired.

CHRIST AND THE DOCTORS

The story of Christ and the Doctors is amply developed in all four cycles. The Virgin's rôle is considerably large, and shows us vividly the parental relation between herself and Christ. We discern here the devoted Mother of the Saviour, worshipful of Him, and heartbroken at His loss. As she and Joseph are journeying back from the yearly festival at Jerusalem, they suddenly realize that Christ is missing. The reaction of Mary is worth quoting. for we can see the conscious restraint of the dramatists in aiming to avoid anything hysterical or even theatrical, and still at the same time preserving a reasonable emotional element, without which the scene would do violence to nature.

TOWNELEY:

Maria: A, dere Ioseph! What is youre red?
     Of oure greatt bayll no boytt may be;
     My hart is heuy as any lede,
     My semely son to I hym se.
     Now haue we soght in every sted,
     Both vp and downe, thise dayes thre;
     And wheder he be whik or dede
     yit wote we not; so woe is me!

York's wording is almost identical and need not be recorded.

position that the Towneley and York were originally one, posits the theory that York, a later revision, came under the influence of the Northern Septenar which sought to soften and scripturalize more and more the biblical drama. See Lyle, " The Original Identity of the York and Towneley Cycles," *Research Publications of the University of Minnesota*, VII (1919), No. 3, 63.

CHESTER:

Maria: Iosephe, husbande leffe and deare,
        our childe is gone upon his way.
        my harte were lighte, and he were here.
        let us goe seeke hym, I thee praie.
        For suddaynly he went away
        and left us both in Ierusalem
        greatly in lyking many a day
        that will be lord over all the realme.

COVENTRY:

Maria: Alas Alas myn hert is wo
        My blyssyd babe a-wey is went
        I wott nevyr whedyr þat he is go
        alas for sorwe myn hert is rent
        Jentyl husbond haue hym sent
        Out on herrande to Any place
        but yf ꝫe knowe were her ys bent
        myn hert for woo A-sondyr wyl race.

There is evidently no overstepping of the Christocentric rôle in any of the above passages. As a matter of fact, the expression is rather tame for such a sudden and momentous accident in the life of a mother. Nevertheless we can see the author's conscious striving after a full effect while at the same time keeping within the limits imposed by the character with whom he is dealing. Each passage is nothing more than an expression of maternal anguish. Although something more hysterical from Mary would be perfectly in order—for dramatic usage—nevertheless her lament is limited and restrained. How manifestly each of the playwrights was capable of depicting very forceful and dramatic hysteria may be inferred readily by a mere glance through the *Massacre* plays.

Coventry has succeeded best in portraying the Mother's grief, while keeping her within the bounds of her Christocentric character:

Maria: Trewly gode spowse not þese days thre
        þerfore myn herte is cast in care
        hym for to seke wher so he be
        in hast good husbonde lete us forth fare.
        I am aferde þat he hath fon
        ffor his grett wyttys and werkys good
        lyke hym of wytt ffor-soth is non
        Euery childe with hym is wroth and wood.[31]

---

[31] Very conceivably the author was acquainted with the infancy legends narrated in the apocryphal gospel of Thomas, according to which the youth-

> Also my babe my blys my blood
> Whedyr art þou þus gon fro me
> my sowle my swetyng my frute myn ffood
> Send me ssum wurd where þat þou be
> Telle me good serys for charyte
> Jhesu my childe þat babe of blysse
> Amonge þis companye dude ȝe hym se
> Ffor godys hyȝ loue telle where he is.

These lines reach a tenderness certainly worthy of the Mother of God. There is nothing frantic in them, yet their mournful and reverent note suggests a significance that the playwright could not impart were he merely trying to exploit the Virgin for dramatic interests.

The meeting of Mother and Child is aptly described in all the plays, and in each, with the exception of Chester, the pathetic strain is continued; that is, Mary mildly reproaches her Son, quite as the Gospel records,[32] drawing the Child's attention to her grief and and to Joseph's. Coventry, from which the following are taken, expresses this meeting with the most detail:

Maria: A dere childe dere chylde why hast þou þus done
             Ffor þe we haue had grett sorwe and care
             thy ffadyr and I thre days haue gone
             Wyde þe to seke of blysse ful bare.
Jhesus: Why haue ȝe sought me with evy fare
             Wete ȝe not wele I muste been
             A-monge hem þat is my faderys ware
             his gostly catel for to ovyrsen.
Maria: ȝour ffaderys wyl must nedys be wrought
             It is most wurthy þat it so be
             ȝitt on ȝour modyr have ȝe sum thought
             And be nevyr more so longe fro me
             As to my thynkynge these days thre
             þat ȝe Absente haue ben A-way
             be more lengere in þer degre
             þan All þe space of xij ȝere day.
Jhesus: Now ffor to plese my modyr mylde
             I xal ȝow folwe with obedyence
             I am ȝour sone and subjecte childe
             and Owe to do ȝow hyȝ reverence

---

ful Jesus often played tricks on His playmates, thereby incurring their resentment and the anger of their parents.

[32] St. Luke, II, 48.

home with ȝow I wyl go hens
Of ȝow clerkys my leve I take
Euery childe xulde with good dyligens
his modyr to plese his owyn wyl forsake.[33]

Chester, on the other hand, and alone of the plays, pictures for us the overjoyed mother, who is too thankful at finding Jesus to give vent to reproach:

Maria: Now blessed be he us hither brought,
in land there lyves none so light!
se where he sitteth we haue sought,
amonge yonder masters, mickle of might!
Wend furth, Ioseph, upon your way
and fetch our sonne, and let us fare,
that sitteth with yonder Doctors gay;
for we haue had of hym great care.
My worthy sonne, to me so deare,
we haue you sought full wonder-wyde;
I am right glad that you be here,
that we haue found you in this tyde.

Once again, therefore, we see depicted the devoted mother, whose grief, however touching and deep, is throughout mildly subdued and clothed in a note of restraint and reverence. Her words entirely befit her rôle. We see again that none of the playwrights has attempted to extend the Virgin's rôle out of its bounds.[34]

[33] Cf.: Sche is so gracyous sche is so mylde
so xulde childyr to fadyr and modyr evyr more.
(Coventry IX, 70)

[34] It is interesting to note the doctrinal accuracy displayed by this Coventry author in regard to Mary. *Secundus Doctor* asks Jesus concerning His Mother; Jesus responds:
Jhesu of Nazareth I am þe same
born of a clene mayd prophetys seyd so
Ysaye seyd þus Ecce virgo
A mayd xal conceyve in clennes a chylde
ȝitt ageyn nature and alkende loo
ffrom all wem of synne pure and vndefylde.
Mary . . .
ys þat clene mayd and here childe am I
þe frute of here wombe xal saue euery manne
Ffrom þe grett dowte of þe ffyndys tormentry.
And *Primus Doctor*, at the end of the play, exclaims:
Fful blyssyd is ȝour modyr hende
of whom ȝe toke ȝour incarnacion.

CHAPTER IV

In this chapter is examined the rôle of Mary, first as Sorrowing Mother, then as Glorified Mother. To arrive at an estimate of the Virgin's status in the Passion plays, it is necessary to study her rôle against their entire background. By that I mean that we cannot come to appreciate her position by glancing merely at what particularly she herself has to say or do; rather attention must be fastened on her in so far as she moves in company with the other characters. I shall demonstrate by this method that the *Planctus Mariae* is eminently Christocentric, and that the emotion with which her plaint is charged always centers upon the fact that Christ is suffering, that He is suffering despite His infinite goodness and innocence. To a certain extent Mary is indeed portrayed emotionally in the Passion scenes, and hardly could be portrayed otherwise; for how else could her motherhood of the Saviour be depicted? Mary grieves, because her Divine Son is undergoing agony. But her anguish is pictured naturally and simply, without any effort at high pathos, and assuredly without producing anything like a maudlin or hysterical effect. To all Christians, the words of the Evangelist, "Now there stood by the cross of Jesus, his mother" (John XIX, 25), have ever connoted a generous but heart-broken Mother of Christ, not a stoical, unfeeling woman. The *Stabat Mater* pictures well this Catholic conception of the Mother of Sorrows, and it is no exaggeration to say that the cyclic dramatists of medieval England have reproduced that conception in its entirety. The emotional picture of Mary they draw for us does not impinge upon her Christocentric status, but truly heightens it, for it shows us the Virgin whose very heart palpitates with the heart of the Suffering Christ. It throws the theme of Christ and Mary, of Mother and Son, into as bold relief as any of the plays hitherto studied.

The Mother and Child theme is vividly carried over into the post-Resurrection Marian plays, wherein the dramatists (of York and Coventry only) show us the Virgin, no longer broken with sorrow,

88

but exulting with the joy of her ascended Son.   Catholics of all times have ever linked up the glories of Mary with her grief.   In the Marian cultus the two are almost supplemental.   Hence in this section I have coupled the study of Mary sorrowing and Mary glorified, just as in the York and Coventry cycles the two themes are quite contiguous.

The Middle English Planctus Mariae

A brief survey of the Middle English *Planctus Mariae* [1] will be in order here before taking up a study of the element in the cyclic plays.   Needless to say, this survey can be at most but a hasty outline.   An attempt at exhaustiveness would carry me too far from the task I have set out to accomplish.   I wish merely to present a background of the *Planctus* in the cyclic plays.   The topic as a whole, I must say, is indeed worth the generous efforts of a student industrious enough to tackle it.   A good deal of work has been done in this field, but it is my opinion that the studies as a whole, laudable as they are, have nevertheless left much untouched.[2]

Roughly speaking, the English *Planctus* was at its height during the period between 1300 and 1500.   It formed an essence of that beautiful poetry (more charming still by reason of its extreme naïveté) which has contributed largely in gaining for England the title " Our Lady's Dowry."   Thien and Taylor have each listed English *Planctus* texts.   The former discusses twenty-seven of these with their variants, while Taylor bases his study upon twenty-five

---

[1] For the sake of clarity I will call attention to the definition of the term *Planctus Mariae*.   As the name indicates, the *Planctus* is subjective of the Mother of God.   Through its medium she records her emotional reactions to the Passion of her Son.   This strictly Marian character places the *Planctus* in a different category from kindred products, such as the *Stabat Mater*, which, while dealing with the grief of the Virgin, does not express that grief in Mary's own wording.

[2] Among the *Planctus* studies may be mentioned in particular: A. Schönbach, *Über die Marienklagen*, Leipsig, 1874; F. Tanquerey, *Plaintes de la Vierge en Anglo-Français*, Paris, 1921; H. Thien, *Über die Englischen Marienklagen*, Kiel Dissertation, 1906; A. Linder, *Plainte de la Vierge*, Upsala, 1898; G. C. Taylor, " The English Planctus Mariae," in *Modern Philology*, IV (1907); Young, " Observations on the Origin of the Medieval Passion Play," *PMLA*, XXV (1910).

texts, beginning with about 1250. Before discussing the work of the latter in its bearing upon the cyclic plays, it may be well to remark that the English *Planctus* is found in four literary forms: the monologue, the dialogue, the lament occurring within the narrative, and the lament as part of the drama. A brief explanation of each seems advisable.

I. The Monologue Form.[3] In this type the Virgin gives touching vent to her sorrow in beholding or recalling the wounds and suffering of her Son. It always takes the form of soliloquy, and oftentimes, as in the piece indicated, Mary addresses herself in compassion:

> Marie, nay but marred I thee call.

II. The Dialogue Form.[4] This type is a dialogue between Christ and His Mother. It is generally characterized by a complete balance of lines. Though not affecting the drama, it belongs to that cast of poetry which is highly dramatic in form.[5] Following is an illustration taken from the poem cited:

> " Stond wel, ounder rode,
> Behold þi child with glade mode;
>   Moder, Bliþe miȝt þou be,"
> " Sone, how may ich bliþe stonde?
> Ich se þine fet, and þine honde,
>   I nayled to þe harde tre."

III. The *Planctus* as a narrative. This ordinarily assumes the form of a monologue, its characteristic being that it occurs in the narrative. Following is a short specimen occurring in the *Assumption of Our Lady:*

> Alas my sone seide heo
> Hu may ihc liue? hu may þis beo?
> Hu may ihc al þis soreȝe iseo?
> Ne cuþe ihc neure of soreȝe noȝt?
> Mi leue sone, wat hastu þoȝt?

---

[3] For an illustration, see " The Compleynte of the Virgin before the Cross," in *Hoccleve's Minor Poems*, ed. by Furnivall, EETS. ES. 61 (1892).

[4] For an illustration, see " Stand wel ounder rode," in *Minor Poems of the Vernon MS.*, ed. by Furnivall, EETS. OS. 117, II (1901).

[5] Taylor, *op. cit.*, pp. 607-608.

Hou schal ihc lyue biþ ute þe?
Leue sone, what seistu me? [6]

IV. The dramatic *Planctus,* which concerns us most. As I have
indicated, this type is represented in all the cycles. Right here I
may remark, before focussing upon any particular plays, that there
is a difference of opinion existing among scholars as to whether or
not the *Planctus* forms the germ of the Passion Plays. Wechssler
was rather emphatic in stating that it does:

> In Italien ist das vulgärsprächliches Drama überhaupt aus den Dicht-
> ungen der Laudesen und zwar speziell aus den Marienklagen erwachsen.
> Und in den Ländern, welche anders als Italien schon zuvor ein vulgärspräch-
> liches geistliches Drama entwickelt haben, beruhen wenigstens die Passions-
> spiele auf unserer Literaturgattung. Im früheren Mittelalter gab es keine
> anderen Dramatisierungen der Leidensgeschichte als die Marienklagen. [7]

Chambers is quite of the same opinion: " The *Planctus* must be
regarded as the starting point of a drama of the Passion." [8] Other
scholars object to the theory. Taylor, commenting upon Wechssler's statement, asks: " Is it not more probable that the play was
based on some model, dramatic or otherwise, and the *Planctus* portion written along with the rest of it? " [9] Young has adduced
several reasons why Wechssler's conjecture is inaccurate. His own
theory (bolstered up by strong evidence) is that " the groundwork
of the Passion Plays is clearly the Gospel account," since the Passion of Christ, according to the evangelists, was read on four days
of the Holy Week. [10] Although this is not the place for an extended
discussion upon the origin of the Passion Play, I feel warranted in
stating my own opinion on the matter. First of all, I cannot
wholly agree with either the theory that, at least in the English
field, the *Planctus* is the seed of the Passion type of play or that
the play is borrowed entirely from the Holy Week liturgy. My
opinion is that the liturgy, the *Planctus* and the very early devotional trends concerning the Passion of Christ, all contributed to

---

[6] Hackauf, E., *Die älteste mittelenglische Version der Assumptio Mariae,*
Berlin, 1902, p. 4.

[7] *Die romanischen Marienklagen,* Halle, 1893, p. 98.

[8] *The Medieval Stage,* II, p. 40.

[9] P. 636.

[10] *Observations on the Origin of the Medieval Passion Play,* PMLA, XXV
(1910), 309.

4

the dramatic framework, but no one element to a preponderant degree. I cannot here bring together all the material required to establish my opinion. However, Kretzmann's table, which he places at the outset of his study, serves to confirm it.[10a]

All this leads us into a focal study of the cyclic *Planctus*. As my aim is to unfold the character of the Virgin's rôle, I will not stop to discuss the various works that are alleged by scholars to be the sources of the *Planctus* in these plays. The sources do not materially affect the line of study in this thesis. It is strictly the Marian element that must be microscoped. For the sake of completeness, however, I am bringing in here the conclusions reached by Taylor and Thien regarding the sources of the Middle English dramatic *Planctus:* Taylor [11] says:

> In York and Chester the *Planctus Mariae* became so thoroughly assimilated with the great body of the play in which they occur that it is not possible to say whether they were once independent lyrics, or were written, along with the rest of the plays, by a dramatist who was familiar with these themes in the religious poetry of the day. In Towneley it seems possible that independent lyric *Planctus* were introduced, without being made to conform thoroughly, as in the case of York and Chester, to the rest of the play. In Hegge they have become more thoroughly part and parcel of the drama than in any of the other plays; the author introduces into them, besides the conventional motives, other turns of thought and fancy, as he sees fit, according to the need of the dramatic situation. In Hegge, however . . . the influence of a particular *Planctus* is to be observed.[12]

Thien's conclusions may be summarized thus:

a. In York the *Planctus* is based principally upon the Tractat [13] of Richard Rolle.

b. In Towneley, it is taken principally from the *Lamentatio,* based upon the *Meditationes* of Bonaventura.

c. In Chester the source is likewise Bonaventura.

[10a] *Op. cit.*

[11] *Op. cit.*, pp. 635-36.

[12] That occurring in the *Betrayal of Christ.* " Mary laments when Mary Magdalene informs her of Christ's capture; in no other English dramatic or non-dramatic verse *Planctus* is Mary introduced speaking at this point of the narrative." (*Ibid.*, p. 624, note.)

[13] Cf. Taylor, p. 609 (note).

d. Coventry receives a triple influence: Bonaventura, the *Tractat,* and *Rosacompassio.*[14]

I shall use *Planctus Plays* simply as a convenient term to denote those plays containing a Marian *Planctus.* The term " Passion Plays " might serve just as well were it not for the fact that the Coventry *Resurrection* and the Towneley *Ascension* also contain a Marian *Planctus.* I have found it much more convenient and, to a certain extent, necessary to deviate from my previous method of procedure. Instead of treating each play separately, I have grouped the whole of the section into one large unit. The Marian element in this division is so scattered that in some instances it would be almost impossible to discuss it in single plays. Such a method would only further complicate a section of the English drama sufficiently involved as it stands. One or two cases of *Planctus,* however, because of the difficulty they present when viewed in their contexts, will have to receive separate discussion.

To arrive at an estimate of Mary's rôle in these plays, we must first of all glance at the *Planctus* themselves, especially in their relation to their contexts. After all, these laments of Mary are really her own words, and are therefore intended by the authors to be an exponent of her character—as they see it. But it may be well to state here that the question of sources will have to receive only a very limited treatment; otherwise, I should have to branch off into a field distinct from the nature of this theme. The *Planctus* is so thoroughly woven into its plays that it would be quite presumptuous to pronounce pontifically upon any definite origins or relations. Taylor's concentrated study in this field, one of the latest and most complete, netted him the following result:

In the discussion of the relationships of the various non-dramatic planctus it was difficult to reach positive conclusions; in the discussion of the dramatic planctus in their relation to the non-dramatic it is just as difficult to obtain definite results. In no case can we say with absolute certainty that any one of the non-dramatic planctus discussed . . . has made its way into any of the miracle plays.[15]

---

[14] This summary of Thien's conclusions is made by Kretzmann, *op. cit.,* p. 109.

[15] *Modern Philology,* IV (1907), 18-19.

In the *Planctus* plays, as in all the others studied thus far, the rôle of the Virgin is purely Christocentric. Here, as elsewhere, my original proposition holds true: Mary's dramatic treatment is accorded her only against the fundamental background of her status of Mother of God, and nowhere is she merely exploited as a figure of dramatic interest. The proof of this proposition shall occupy the remainder of this section. But in connection with this I have another observation to make, namely, that in the *Planctus* plays Mary is not such a focal figure as she has hitherto been. This fact, as I intend to show, emphasizes the Christocentricity of her rôle. The plays are devoted to the Passion of Christ, and the sufferings of the Saviour are stressed wherever possible. But although Mary is not a focal figure to her former extent, there are still the customary reverence, the cautious restraint and the delicate consideration that have hitherto characterized her. Another thing points to her Christocentric rôle: I mean the fact that, whereas the structure of her *Planctus* has much in common with the plaints of Magdalene, John, the three Marys, Nicodemus and Joseph of Arimathea, thus indicating that she, with them, is introduced primarily to emphasize the tragedy of Christ's Passion, nevertheless the emphasis in her *Planctus* rests upon the fact that she is Mother of the Suffering Saviour. And be it noted that I wish here in using the expression, Mother of the Saviour, to imply that the emphasis is not so much on the Mother as on the Saviour. In other words her rôle is not the development of the mother-in-distress idea for its own sake, but rather a medium through which attention is brought to the Saviour. Again, I shall attempt to prove that one of the main purposes of the *Planctus* in these plays is to expound the doctrinal interpretation of the mystery of the Redemption. Likewise I shall point out places in which the playwrights seem to have modelled their *Planctus* (not only of Mary, but of the other characters mentioned, including even Christ), upon the "contrast" scheme of the *Reproaches* that are chanted on Good Friday during the Adoration of the Cross. Several illustrations will be given with a view to making the matter clear.

The parallels that follow below are selected more or less at random, and by no means exhaust the full stock that lies so widely interspersed among the four cycles. I have simply singled out as many as I thought sufficient to illustrate the usual modes of expression accorded Mary among the plays, and at the same time to show that her rôle receives no dramatic specialization; that is, there is nowhere any indication that the dramatists were trying to make her a stellar figure. The selections I give, of course, bespeak emotion, emotion aroused in a devoted Mother at the sight of her Son's agonies. This is not a dramatic liberty, since it really accentuates the Christocentric character of the Virgin. It clearly emphasizes her status of Mother of the Suffering Saviour, and its ultimate effect is to direct attention to the Suffering Saviour Himself. We discern here the *Mater Dolorosa* in her true Catholic conception. It is well to remember the fact that Catholics venerate the Sorrowful Mother, not with the sympathy commonly tendered the ordinary woman in distress over the death of a dear son, but with a piety that hinges upon her motherhood of the Man of Sorrows. To help make clear that that is the view of Catholicism, I can hardly do better than quote a collect from the Mass of the seven sorrows of the Blessed Virgin Mary, occurring in the Roman Missal on the Friday after Passion Sunday:

O God, in whose Passion the sword of sorrow foretold by Simeon did pierce the most sweet soul of the glorious Mary, Virgin and mother: grant, in thy mercy, that we, who reverently call to mind her anguish and suffering, may, through the glorious merits and intercession of all the saints who faithfully stood by the cross,[16] obtain the blessed fruit of thine own Passion.[17]

I shall try to show that the dramatists, working in the spirit of that collect, were building not around the Virgin, but Christ. The motherly consternation with which some of Mary's utterances are charged does not impair her Christocentric status, since this emo-

[16] Referring to St. John, chapter 19, verse 25: "Now there stood by the cross of Jesus, His mother . . . " This is also contained in the Introit of the Mass.

[17] The first mention of a feast in honor of Our Lady's sorrows occurs in 1433, when the Council of Cologne instituted the feast of the Anguish and Sorrow of the Blessed Virgin Mary. Not until toward the end of the sixteenth century did it spread over southern Europe. (See F. Holweck, "Sorrows of the B. V. M.," in *Catholic Encyclopedia*, XIV (1913), 152.) I have not been able to determine when this collect was composed.

tion is primarily directed and subordinated to the agonies of Christ. The burden of every Marian *Planctus* in the plays consists of two essential elements: an expression of deep compassion for Christ, and an expression of restrained motherly grief. The latter element is always subordinated to the former, and always throws the divine maternity into relief. There is nothing maudlin or hysterical to it. It is merely a beautifully charged motherly emotion, modestly manifesting itself, but not commanding the chief attention. Indeed, this is the distinguishing feature of Mary's *Planctus* in the cycles, the only feature that lifts her rôle above that of her fellow characters, who, as I shall show, are simply foils whereby to heighten the tragedy of the Passion. Wherever the Virgin's *Planctus* is not riveted upon the Suffering Christ, wherever it becomes self-commiserative, the Mother of Christ idea rises and becomes the chief reason why she grieves. Mary as a detached dramatic figure does not appear in these plays. Her Christocentric status incessantly enshrouds her rôle.

The following sets of paraphrased parallels,[18] picked at random, will illustrate what I mean. Group A contains the theme in which Mary speaks of her heart. Studied apart from their contexts, these extracts might appear to be dramatic usages; hence, in order to present their real setting I have also inserted in italics those portions of the contexts which give the essential coloring. Group B, presenting the theme in which Mary commiserates herself, also brings out the Christocentric basis of her lament. Similarly with C and D, in which the Virgin respectively calls on death and wonders why her Child, who is innocence itself, should be so cruelly treated by those whom He has always helped. I am citing these extracts for two reasons. The first is to show that there are standard modes of *Planctus* throughout the cycles, indicating, by their very commonness, that the dramatists were certainly not attempting a construction upon Mary's rôle such as would set her up as a dramatic feature. Secondly, I wish to show that in all these parallels the *Planctus* fastens attention, not on Mary, but on Christ. The human element in each group of citations cannot be

---

[18] Since my aim is to present only the similarities in idea, I have thought it sufficient to paraphrase and compress, rather than to quote directly and fully.

construed into distinct attempts to set up Mary as a detached dramatic figure, since (as the italics indicate) her emotion is aroused chiefly over Christ. Again I ask the reader to note how the italics (which are mine) indicate the shift of interest to Christ.

A.

Theme: Mary speaks of her heart.

My heart is cold as stone at these woeful tidings. Would that it break!
Jesus, Jesus, Jesus, Jesus, why do You suffer these things? (C. XXVIII.)
Alas, my dear Child is dead. Ah, my heart, why do you beat now? (C. XXXII.)
Weep with me for my Child, the best born. My heart is stiff as stone! (T. XXIII.)
Now, Son Jesus, my heart is heavy as lead. (Y. XXXVI.)

B.

Theme: Mary commiserates herself.

Never did *a mother* suffer such woe, *see her Child so despoiled!* (C. XXXIV.)
There was never a woman more sorrowful than I *when I saw my Son nailed upon the tree!* (C. XXXV.)
My sorrow, *dear Son, at seeing Thee,* is more than tongue may tell. (T. XXIII.)

C.

Theme: Mary calls upon death.

Ah, my good Lord, my Son so sweet, is there no other death to Thee now meet? Ah, death, why wilt thou not kill me? Let me hang upon the tree *with my Son!* (C. XXXII.)
Let me die, *Son, for Your sake.* Thieves, slay me *and let my Son* go. (Ch. XVI.)
Alas, that I should live *to see my Son in this pain!*—I think that I have lived too long thus to see *my Son* bleed! (T. XXIII.)

D.

Theme: Mary is perplexed why the innocence of her Son should be so cruelly repaid.

(The Christocentricity of these laments is too obvious to be singled out by italics.)

Ah, Jesus, why should You suffer these things, who have ever
been so good?—Ah, Father, why should Thy Son, who was
always so good, gentle, kind, pitiful and obedient, now suffer
these things? (C. XXVIII.)
You have been gracious to others, have pity on Yourself!
(T. XXII.)
Alas, He hangs like a thief, and He never trespassed! (Y.
XXVI.)

Clearly there is no attempt to dramatize the Virgin as a detached
figure. Her function is to testify to the tragedy of the Passion.
The only element that distinguishes her rôle is itself Christocentric
—the divine maternity. The following are specimens of *Planctus*
from various other characters, cited for the purpose of showing
their manifest similarity in function to the laments of the Virgin:

1st mulier:
Alas, Jesus, woe is me, that You who never had fault should
be so despoiled!

2nd mulier:
Ah! here is a wicked sight, that Jesus, who is so good, should
receive such treatment! (C. XXXII.)

Nicodemus:
Alas, what a sight! The Lord who never sinned is nailed on
a tree! (C. XXXIV.)

2nd Mary:
Alas, He that was ever lovely and good now suffers this sinful
treatment!

3rd Mary:
This sign shall bear witness to all people, how God's peerless
Son underwent peerless pain. (Y. XXXIV.)

Joseph of Arimathea:
Let all mankind mark: no falseness could they find in Him,
yet they killed Him. (Y. XXXVI.)

Mary Magdalen:
Jesus that is so good they now heap grief upon. (Y. XXII.)

John:
Alas! to me and to many others was thy Son a good Master.
(T. XXIII.)

Mary Magdalen:

Alas! how should my heart be light when I see my seemly Lord so torn and disfigured—He who never did man greviously!

Maria Jacobia:

Alas, sorrow sets me sore! Jesus is dying, who gave life to the dead!

Joseph of Arimathea:

What hearts have ye, to slay this Man who never did amiss? (Ch. XVII.)

John:

Alas! for my Master, who, come to mend man's misdeeds, is falsely accused and condemned! (Y. XXXIV.)

2nd Mary:

Those whom He minded most now hasten to kill Him! (Y. XXXIV.)

Prima Maria:

Alas! so many sick has He saved, and now He is made go this way to be killed! Ch. XVII.)

It will be seen at a glance that the function of these laments and those of Mary is one and the same, to concentrate attention upon the Passion of Christ. Note especially the scheme of contrast—a very effective way indeed to bring out the depth of Christ's sufferings and goodness: " He dies, who raised the dead; " " They slay this Man, who never did amiss; " " You have been gracious to others, have pity on Yourself;" etc. This framework is particularly evident in Group D of Mary's *Planctus*. Doubtless it was inspired by the contrast scheme of the Sarum Missal *Reproaches*,[19] sung during the Adoration of the Cross on Good Friday. Just how they may have come to inspire many of the *Planctus* in the English medieval cyclic plays is a question which I must leave rest; at any rate, I have come across what might almost be termed a paraphrase of these *Reproaches* in the *Stanzaic Life of Christ*.[20] In fact the poet quotes portions of the Sarum *Reproaches* for his text. The words of Christ from the Cross in the Towneley Crucifixion

[19] *The Sarum Missal*, F. W. Legg, ed., Oxford, 1916, pp. 112-113.
[20] Pp. 184-188.

(XXIII) also compel belief in the influence of the *Reproaches* upon them. At any rate, though we must let the problem pass as something lying outside this work, still, if it could be decisively proved that the laments of both Mary and her fellow-characters in the cyclic plays are built upon the contrast-framework of the Sarum *Reproaches,* we should have additional strong evidence of the Christocentricity of the Virgin's rôle in these plays.

However, further persuasive evidence is not lacking. I refer to the fact that Mary powerfully enhances the Christocentric aspect of these Passion plays by frequently provoking a doctrinal exposition of the mystery of the redemption. Generally it is St. John who does the explaining, and it is always an attempt to comfort the Virgin. In places Jesus delivers these expositions to her from the Cross, and at times she herself in monologue declares the meaning of her Son's agonies. Following are random instances paraphrased. Note particularly the constant convergence to Christ, the doctrinal aspect, and the complete absence of striving after dramatic effect:

Mary:

Why, gracious Father, must Jesus suffer? Cannot man be saved in any other way? Yet, Father, Thou shalt comfort my woe, when man is saved and brought to a good end. Dear Son, You are so full of mercy that You will not spare Yourself, out of love for mankind. (C. XXVIII.)

Jesus (in answer to Mary's lament):

Woman, know that the Father sent Me to take this manhood of thee and then to pay Adam's ransom and deliver mankind from the bondage of the devil. Do not let these sufferings of Mine displease you, then, Mother. (C. XXXII.)

John (in answer to Mary's lament):

Change your thought, blessed Maid, for by His own will are these sufferings wrought. I tell you, blessed Lady, that did He not die, we should all go to hell. But by His suffering death for our trespasses we have grace to dwell with Him in Heaven.

Mary replies:

Dear friend, well do I know this, that He now buys us to His bliss. (C. XXXII.)

Mary:

Here is my innocent dead Child! Ah, Father of Heaven, it should be so. (C. XXXIV.)

The *Resurrection* play of the Coventry cycle shows Mary again testifying, this time in a joyful strain, to the mystery of the Redemption.

Mary:

Ah! dear Son! Blessed be that precious blood which has saved mankind. All men may now have glee. My Child has suffered and brought all to bliss! (C. XXXV.)

Jesus (in answer to Mary's lament):

Mother, I must die on the cross and rise on the third day. Man's soul that I forever love I must redeem and bring into Heaven for all time. (T. XXII.)

John (in answer to Mary's lament):

But, Lady, thy Son suffers of His own will, and shall ransom mankind and save us from sorrow. (T. XXIII.)

Mary (calling to Christ on the Cross):

Sweet Son, what wonder is this that Thou art brought to such suffering?

John answers her:

Remember, My Master told us that He should die on a tree, and on the third day, rise again. He will lift our bale. His love makes Him suffer for us. (T. XXIII.)

Jesus (answering Mary's lament):

My Mother mild, change thy mood. These sharp pains that I suffer here are endured because My Father wills that I save mankind from the fiend. (T. XXIII.)

John (answering Mary's lament):

Comfort thee now, sweet, for when He has fulfilled these things of prophecy, He shall rise again in three days. (Ch. XVII.)

Jesus (answering Mary's lament):

Do not weep, for I am carrying out My Father's will by allowing My body to be tortured, and thus deliver mankind. (Y. XXXVI.)

The Christocentric character of Mary's rôle is manifest in all these instances. Nowhere does she stand out apart from the others, except, as I have noted, in those places where her motherhood of the Suffering Christ is emphasized.

One last point remains, a point which really is obvious from the evidence I have already presented, but which may be treated a trifle further without too much redundancy. I mean the fact that Mary is nowhere exploited for dramatic interests. Of all the plays up and down the cycles, none offers richer opportunities for extending Mary's rôle than do these *Planctus* plays. The very nature of the plays — their scenes of conflict, their tragic significances — must have sorely tempted the imagination of the playwrights as they assigned Mary her rôle. As it is, there is abundant free play of the pen: Pilate's ranting and his cunning; the struggle to get Simon to carry Christ's cross; the dream of Pilate's wife; the realistic earnestness of the soldiers in the crucifixion scene in York and Towneley; the squabble over the Saviour's seamless coat—these testify to the lively imagination of the various authors and to their readiness to make use of the apocrypha. Just why they restrain themselves when dealing with Mary is clear. Try to picture with what avidity these playwrights would have gone to work on St. Joseph's rôle if the Gospel had included him in the narrative of Christ's Passion!

Before finishing this section I want to call attention to the peculiarity of the Marian *Planctus* in the Coventry *Betrayal* (XXVIII, lines 1053-1084). Mary Magdalen announces the capture of Christ to His Mother. The latter immediately breaks into a lament which, because of certain lines, would first of all appear to belong to a scene more connected with Christ's physical suffering, for example the scourging, the buffeting, the procession to Calvary or the Crucifixion:

> A jhesu, jhesu, jhesu, jhesu
> Why xuld ȝe sofere þis trybulacyon and Advercyte . . .
> Where-fore þan xuld ȝe sofer þis gret peyn . . .
> . . . now þe bryth colour of his face doth fade.
> A good fadyr why woldyst þat þin owyn dere sone xal sofre
>   Al þis . . .

Besides suggesting misplacement, this *Planctus* offers another peculiarity. Mary, wondering why her Son should suffer " þis gret peyn " makes the startling remark:

I suppoce veryly it is for þe tresspace of me
And I wyst þat myn hert xuld cleve on tweyn.
Ffor þese langowrys may I susteyn
Þe swerd of sorwe hath so thyrlyd my meende
Alas what may I do Alas what may I seyn
Þese prongys myn herte A-sondyr þei do rende.

Of course we immediately discern here the mistaken interpretation that was once given to Simeon's utterance, in which he told Mary that a sword should pierce her heart.[21] But the surprising thing is that the interpretation finds its way here at all. I have not been able to find any other instance in any of the cycles where the " sword " is interpreted as a sin of the Virgin's. Surely the playwright could not have meant this when he put it down. I say so because just a few lines above he introduces Mary Magdalen hailing the Blessed Virgin as ' immaculate mother: "

O in-maculate modyr of all women most meke
O devowtest in holy medytacion evyr A-bydyng . . .

Why, then, does he immediately after speak of her as having sinned? The idea of attaching guilt to the Mother of God, even in such a slight way as is done here, flies in the face of all the treatment accorded Mary, not merely in the Coventry cycle, but throughout the entire English medieval drama. I think this passage can easily be explained on the assumption that the playwright was simply fitting in a current Marian *Planctus*.[22] Its very position—at the end of the play—would seem to indicate that our author was working under pressure, looking for a *Planctus* that must be inserted hastily. This supposition is all the more probable when we consider—as I have pointed out above—that the lament must have been written for a more painful scene of Christ's Passion. But the *Betrayal* has no scene in which Christ is involved in physical suffering. There is not even an element of violence, except for Peter's striking off the ear of Malchus and the binding of Christ by the Jews. At any rate, we can easily see that the aim of the author was to add an element that would emphasize the

[21] I refer to the interpretation which construes the " sword " into a future sin of doubt in Mary. See p. 79 of this essay.

[22] I have been unable, however, to trace this lament to any current *Planctus*.

sufferings of Christ. Were his aim to focus the Virgin, we should
find it difficult to explain why he did not revise that curious
Planctus.

All in all then, it appears to be clear that the rôle of Mary in
these *Planctus* plays is purely Christocentric. We have seen that
she is introduced to underline the Passion of her Son, and that her
rôle is subject to the same restraint that we have hitherto observed.
I ought to remark that Mary's *Planctus* in the Cornish Passion
follows the same trend that I have been describing.[23] It is Christocentric, stressing the doctrinal part of the Redemption (by John's
words of comfort, as in the cycles), and in no way opening her rôle
to dramatic liberties.

Up to this point in the present chapter, I have been dealing with
the rôle of Mary Sorrowing. A word of transition is necessary
before taking up her rôle in the following three plays, which portray her as Glorified Mother. These plays are of a very devotional
character. If any treatment of them appears cursory, it is because
their sameness, their devotional content, and their dramatic lean-
ness offer very little room for comment. Compared with the other
Marian plays we have been considering these three do not present
any extraordinary phases of interest. This lack of dramatic interest is due primarily to the fact that the plays are too unnatural
and tenuous. They strive to project the mundane into the
heavenly. They are too lacking in human experience. Consequently, it is not at all surprising that what we normally consider
of human dramatic worth should have little chance of representation here. Indeed, even Rosetti's attempt, in *The Blessed Damo-
zel,* to carry over human mundane experiences into the world beyond the grave, is generally viewed, even by the more independent
critics, as a source of wonder—also of suspicion. Even if Milton,
too, attempts quite successfully to justify the ways of God to man,
he does not get beyond the range of mundane experience. Dante,
of course, does carry us to the world beyond, but it is always from
the anthropomorphic point of view. These are the thoughts we
should keep in mind as we study the plays of the glorification.

[23] *The Ancient Cornish Drama*, I, ed. E. Norris. Oxford, 1859, 429, 457,
473.

Like the *Planctus* plays, they strive, as bravely as they can, in consonance with the Christian mind, to bring a measure of concreteness to facts having to do with the kingdom that is to come. Instead of embracing the theme of Christ and His Mother in anguish, they depict Christ and His Mother in glory.

THE DEATH OF MARY

Gabriel, in York's *Death of Mary,* comes from Heaven to tell Mary that she has but three days to live. Note the titles he bestows upon her: " myghfull Marie, Godis modir so mylde, root of all reste, floure and frewte not fadid nor filyd, salue to all synnefull." This salutation really sounds the keynote of the play, as far as the Virgin-rôle is concerned. It seems to banish the possibility of exploitation. The devotional atmosphere is at once created, and the reference to Mary as " Godis modir so mylde " immediately suggests the Christocentricity of her rôle. After Gabriel finishes his message, Mary exclaims:

> I thanke my sone semely of all his sandis sere,
> Vn-to hym lastandly be ay louyng,
> Þat me þus worþely wolde menske on þis manere,
> And to his bigly blisse my bones for to bringe

A little while later she tells John that her " swete sone " said she would die. And when, at her prayer, several other apostles suddenly appear in her room to assist her at death, she utters the thanksgiving:

> Jesu, my darlyng þat ding is, and dere,
> I thanke þe my dere sone of þi grete grace

As Mary is dying, York introduces an apocryphal element not found in Coventry's *Assumption.* Two Jews implore her prayers for themselves and for their sins. They base their appeal on the irresistible ground that she is of their race. As *Secundus Judaeus* puts it,

> Sen þou lady come of oure kynne,
> þou helpe vs nowe, þou veray virginne,
> Þat we may be broght vnto blisse.

Undoubtedly, the author intends to recall the intercessory power of Mary, for she announces that she prays for her kinsfolk, for all

who call on her in storms at sea, for all who are oppressed or in
need, and especially for women in childbirth. However, the
dramatist makes it clear where this power of intercession comes
from. He shows us the Mother interceding with her Son:

> Jesus, my sone, for my sake beseke I þe þis,
> As þou arte gracious and grete God, þou graunte me my grace!

Moreover, she constantly calls Him her Son: " my blissid barne,"
" my sone, for my sake . . . ," " my bliste barne," " socoure þame
sone." Jesus appears and assures her of the power of her prayers:

> Marie, my modir, thurgh þe myght nowe of me,
> For to make þe in mynde with mirthe to be mending,
> Þyne asking all haly here heete I nowe þe.

Her remaining rôle is pronouncedly clear upon this aspect of
Mother and Son. Again, in Scene II, we hear Christ:

> Myne aungellis . . .
> . . . I will þat ȝe wende,
> And bringe me my modir to þe highest of heuene . . .
> My modir schall myldely be me
> Sitte nexte þe high Trinite,
> And neuere in two to be twynnand.

The Virgin's rôle here is evidently thoroughly Christocentric, for
she is constantly associated with her Son. Her motherhood of
Christ is emphasized, even by Christ Himself. And the playwright
also sees an opportunity to stress her intercessory power, being careful to base it upon her prerogative. This idea has ever been popular
among Catholic theologians and mystics, particularly from the time
of St. Bernard. Theologians tend more and more unanimously to
say that even grace comes to us through Mary.[23a] And always, as
in the medieval English drama, this intercessory power derives itself
from the fact that she is Mother of the Saviour. The belief is that
just as Christ Himself came to us through Mary, so likewise do all
blessings from Christ pass first through her hands. That is why,
in the Coventry *Assumption,* we hear the archangel Michael
remarking:

> Hefne and erthe now injoye may ye
> Ffor god throw mary is mad mannys frend.

[23a] See Tanquery, *The Spiritual Life,* p. 85.

The Assumption and Coronation

In both cycles in which the play occurs—York and Coventry— the treatment of Mary's Assumption into Heaven after death is very similar. The tradition of the Assumption goes back to very early times. I need not digress into the subject of origins, for it is amply discussed by G. McKnight in his introduction to the Assumption poem.[24] This play seems to be the crowning Christocentric play of all the cycles. From beginning to end the relations of Jesus and Mary—relations here depicted touchingly and vividly— remain in focus. Jesus Himself is introduced frequently, and the lavish encomiums heaped upon Mary by the apostles all center around her status of Mother of Christ. There is a wonderful reverence paid to Mary. This play, in both cycles, seems to have the deepest devotional flavor of all the Marian plays. The nearest approach to it comes in the Coventry *Mary in the Temple*.

Here in this Coventry play we see her in the temple, glorifying her Son and asking that He take her into His presence:

O hye wysdam . . .
that it lyst you of me sympilest to take here humanite . . .
and gloryous lord and sone yif it like youre benygnyte . . .
syn ye wern born god and man of my bodye
to desyre yowre presens that were oure ferste formacyon.

Christ answers her, calling her " sweet mother," and says that her holy heart and her love are upon Him. Wherefore He sends an angel to tell her that within three days she shall be with Him. The salutation of *Angelus* is a beautiful panegyric:

Heyl excellent prynces mary most pure
Heyl radyant sterre the sunne is not so bryth
Heyl moder of mercy and mayde most mure
the blessyng that god yaf Jacob vp on you now is lyth.[25]

He announces that she shall ascend to Heaven where " my god youre sone is." Mary intimates that she would like to die without the devil being near, but *Angelus* immediately rejoins:

[24] G. McKnight, *King Horn Floriz and Blauncheflur, The Assumption of Our Lady*, EETS. OS. 14 (1866), xlix ff. See also L. Smith, *York Mystery Plays*, Introd., xlii.
[25] See Taylor, *Modern Philology*, V (1907), 20.

> What nedith it to fere you empres so hende
> syn be the fruth of youre body was convycte his vyolens
> that horible serpent dar not nyhyn youre kende

When all the apostles wonderingly find themselves transported to
Mary's chamber, she solves their quandary by telling them that

> Tho my sone jhesu of his hye pete
> sent to me an aungyl and thus he sayd
> that the thredde nyth I schuld assende to my sone in deite
> thanne to haue youre presence brether hertly I prayed
> And thus at my request god hath you sent me.

Follows a conversation between Mary and *Dominus,* in which she
addresses Christ as " swete sone Jhesu," " Jhesu sone and god of
mercy." Christ in turn calls her " my moder, here of whom I dede
seke." Their conversation then continues in Latin, *Dominus* speaking in terms of the *Canticles* and Mary in terms of the *Magnificat.*
The Lord later addresses her, after her death:

> Go thanne blyssid soule to that body ageyn . . .
> tabernacle of Joye vessel of lyf hefnely temple to reyn
> ye schal haue the blysse wyth me moder that hath non ende
> Ffor as ye were clene in erthe of alle synnys greyn
> so schul ye reyne in hefne clennest in mend . . .
> yow to worchepe moder it likyth the hol trinyte
> Wherfore I crowne you here in this kyndam of glory
> of alle my chosyn thus schul ye clepyd be
> qwen of hefne and moder of mercy.

York's account likewise gives the Marian rôle this thoroughly
Christocentric aspect. *Jesus* opens the play, telling us that it were
highly unfitting not to take to Heaven the body of His Mother, the
body that gave Him flesh and blood. A deputed *Angelus* pays this
tribute to her:

> Hayle! þe doughtir of blissid Anne,
> Þe which consayued thurgh þe holy goste,
> And þou brought forthe both god and manne,
> The whiche felled doune þe fendis boste.

The other angels echo this sentiment, stressing her motherhood of
Christ. Upon reaching Heaven she hails the Saviour, calling Him
" Jesu my sone " several times and thanking Him. He likewise
addresses her as " mother bright." The whole play breathes of deep
devotion to Christ and His Mother.

The Appearance of Our Lady to Thomas

The *Appearance of Our Lady to Thomas,* found only in the York collection, echoes the devotional tone of the *Death of Mary,* and her assumption and coronation. Thomas, on his way from India, ruefully mourns the death of Christ and the ingratitude of the Jews who killed Him. Suddenly he finds himself miraculously transported to the Vale of Jehoshaphat in Judea. His amazement subsides into fatigue, so he decides to lie down and rest. Meanwhile Mary appears to him in a vision, angels singing before her. They eulogize her with prettiest titles: " Maiden and Mother," " Lily, Most Chaste," " Ripe Rose Redolent," " Dove," " Turtle," " Tabernacle and Temple," " Full Goodley in Grace," " Chosen Childe," " Mary Mild," " Flower Undefiled." Thomas is enraptured at the vision, and Mary tells him that she now abides in bliss with her Son. Now is the apostle's turn to praise her: " Gentlest of the Jews," "Wealth of the World," " Seat of Salvation." Of course there can be no difficulty in recognizing with Taylor [26] that lyrics such as we see in these plays are direct borrowings and paraphrasings of current devotional lyrics. Nevertheless we readily discern that their adaptation supposes an out-and-out Christocentric rôle for the Virgin. The delicacy and reverence with which the legend is dramatized betoken consummate deliberation. That is why these latter Marian plays seem not to lie outside the possibility of having been set up by ecclesiastical composers.

Return now to the play in hand. Mary tells Thomas of her assumption, body and soul, into Heaven, and desires him to inform the other apostles. Poor Thomas, aware of his own incredulity when the others informed him of the Saviour's resurrection, now fears to attempt passing his word upon his fellow-laborers. Mary seeks to encourage him, however, and as a last resort gives him her girdle as a token whereby to reassure the apostles. Thomas is profuse in his thanks and utters another long eulogy of beautiful titles. She also tells the happy man that she is especially desirous of helping all the needy who call upon her:

---

[26] *Ibid.,* p. 16 ff.

Thomas, . . .
. . . in siȝtte of my sone . . .
Shall I knele to þat comely with croune;
Þat what dispaire be dale or be doune
With pitevous playnte in perellis will pray me,
If he synke or swete, in swelte or in swoune,
I schall sewe to my souerayne sone for to say me.
He schall graunte þame þer grace,
Be it manne in his mournyng,
Or womanne in childinge,
All þes to be helpinge,
Þat prince schall I praye in þat place.

This last, of course, is a repetition of Mary's intercessory power, but note especially how her status of Mother of Christ is woven in.

A Supplementary Word

The question may arise, in connection with this study of the Virgin's rôle: Does not the frequent presence of apocrypha in many Marian plays throughout the cycles impinge upon the Virgin's Christocentric status? Does it not suggest a neglect of that status in favor of dramatic embroidery? In other words, does not the non-scriptural material affecting the Virgin's rôle, in such plays as the Coventry *Trial of Joseph and Mary,* or the *Betrothal of Mary* in the same cycle, seem inconsistent with the respect owing to the canonical records of Mary, and hence appear introduced into the plays simply for theatrical purposes, without regard to the exalted character of the Virgin? An answer to this question demands at least a cursory glance at antecedent facts anent the element of apocrypha in the legends of the English people. Such a glance may show, with tolerable accuracy, how the apocrypha found their way into the English Medieval Mysteries. It will at least show, I hope, that the apocrypha connected with the Virgin's rôle do not minimize her Christocentric status.

To begin with, many of the apocryphal elements in the Mysteries are traditions long sanctioned by the Church. In the Marian cultus these traditions are the immaculate conception, the presentation in the temple, the betrothal, and the assumption into Heaven. None of the episodes is mentioned in the canonical records; yet, from early times they have formed the nucleus of the

Catholic Marian cultus. Readily, then, do we perceive that their presence in connection with the Virgin-rôle holds nothing inconsistent with the Christocentric status. Wherever they occur in the plays, they effect no departure from the reverent treatment accorded Mary. In the *Betrothal,* for example, we saw nothing but a characteristic delicacy and restraint in the handling of Mary's rôle; Joseph, whose reluctance to marry is provided in the apocryphal account (*Pseudo-Matthew,* VIII), rehearses that reluctance in a very robust and exaggerated way on the Coventry stage, while Mary's modesty and meekness on this occasion as future Mother of God, are carefully delineated and expanded into a beautiful picture, although they receive little or no emphasis in *Pseudo-Matthew.* But does the same argument hold for those legends which do not enter officially into Catholic tradition, such as the story of the midwives, or the *Trial of Joseph and Mary?* Regarding the midwives, or *obstetrices* episode, it certainly belonged to an early liturgical tradition, for it is found in the Rouen liturgical drama known as the *Officium Pastorum,* the *obstetrices* being impersonated by two priests.[27] Again in the Rouen *Officium Stellae* two priests in dalmatics appear to be identical with the *obstetrices* of the *Officium Pastorum.*[28] It is most probable, therefore, that this episode entered the Mystery Nativity plays as a liturgical tradition rather than as a direct borrowing from current transcriptions of the apocrypha. The story was doubtless part of those devotional legends which were so lovable to the English at large. I do not, however, assign this love of pious lore entirely to what ten Brink calls " a growing passion for authorship, a waning erudition and an increasing belief in the miraculous." [29] I prefer to believe that the *obstetrices* tradition, together with kindred traditions calculated to enkindle the piety of the laity, received at least the tacit approbation of ecclesiastical authorities. Doubtless such legends as the *obstetrices* and the *Trial of Joseph and Mary,* though both of them at bottom apocryphal, helped to illustrate and vivify many

[27] Chambers, *The Medieval Stage,* II, p. 41.
[28] *Ibid.,* p. 46.
[29] *History of English Literature* (Fourteenth Century to Surrey), tr. by Brandl, New York, 1896.

a sermon or homily aiming to extol the virgin birth. Wells has sketched a history of how the English homily gradually incorporated legendary [30] material into its scriptural and commentary elements, thus transmitting to a receptive congregation many an embellished life of a saint, or non-canonical pictures out of the lives of Christ and the Virgin.[31] Thus, among English homilies of the twelfth century we find an account of the Virgin's assumption.[32] The same theme is developed in the *Blickling Homilies* [33] of the tenth century. And we find discussions upon the conception of Mary in *Mirk's Festial*,[34] as also in several other less noteworthy homilies, in manuscript, listed and described by Wells.[35] It seems most probable, then, that the apocrypha in the Mysteries were a matter of pious tradition, conveyed to the workaday folk in the form of sermon or homily. It is hard to imagine that, of the large stock of Early and Middle English homilies unknown to us, many did not embody numerous other apocryphal themes. It is true that the apocryphal gospels themselves are,

[30] By "legendary" I do not mean fictitious. The word "legend" originally denoted a reading from a saint's life (*New Standard Dictionary*). The following definition of a saint's legend is worthy of note: "The saint's legend is a biographical narrative, of whatever origin circumstances may dictate, written in whatever medium may be convenient, concerned as to substance with the life, death, and miracles of some person worthy to be considered a leader in the cause of righteousness; and, whether fictitious or historically true, calculated to glorify the memory of its subject" (Gerould, *Saints' Legends*, p. 5). In the early Church it was sufficient to have the local calendar read without narrative attachment to recall to the minds of the worshippers the deeds of those who had lived and suffered for the true belief. In this way such calendars and martyrologies came into use as part of the services of the Church (*Ibid.*, p. 13). The apocryphal stories emphasized the humanity of Christ, while their addition to the life of the Virgin brought into relief her position of Mother of God, and thus became increasingly popular as her cult grew. Gerould observes that the cult and legends of Mary influenced profoundly the legendary writings of Middle English (p. 150).

[31] *A Manual of the Writings in Middle English* (1050-1400), New Haven, 1916, pp. 285-287.

[32] Ed. Morris, *Old English Homilies* (second series), EETS. OS. 53 (1873).

[33] Ed. Morris, EETS. OS. 58, 63 (1874, 1876).

[34] Ed. Erbe, EETS. ES. 96 (1905).

[35] *Loc. cit.*, p. 330.

as far as research has determined, the ultimate sources of such themes as the *Betrothal of Mary,* the *obstetrices* and the *Trial of Joseph and Mary.*[36] Nevertheless, does it not appear most probable that these themes became circulatory with the years, interweaving themselves with the pious trends of the people? A story like the *Trial of Joseph and Mary* must have enlivened an otherwise dull sermon on the incarnation. Not that the congregation identified such a story with Scripture. Craig is hardly precise in stating that, "The people of England in 1468 did not draw a very sharp distinction between those stories which were definitely in the Bible and those generally accepted as 'gospel truth.'"[37] We can hardly imagine such credulity in a Catholic people who generally accepted what the Church accepted, and rejected what she rejected. The question of their believing in these illustrative addenda to scriptural facts was a matter depending no doubt on personal devotion; and depending more particularly on the attitude of the Church, whether she saw fit to approve or condemn or whether she chose to make no pronouncement at all. Witness how Catholics to-day, with the sanction of the Church, believe that the Virgin, after her assumption, was crowned Queen of Heaven and Earth. No Catholic, in his piety, identifies this tradition with Scripture, although he hold it equally true with Scripture. At any rate, much legendary material, though ultimately founded on the apocrypha, was brought into the devotional life of the early and medieval English. By just what ways it came to England and expanded, is a matter that has continued obscure. It may have entered with, or grown out of, the practice of commemorating the saints by means of illustrated homilies.

It had long been a national custom in France to recite rhymed lives of the saints, either during Mass, or, when the Roman Curia had to forbid this, at least during the evening service. In England the way for this custom was prepared by Aelfric's alliterative homilies, and it found speedy

---

[36] Greg (*Bibliographical and Textual Problems of the English Miracle Cycles,* pp. 76-77-78) observes that the most probable immediate sources of the traditions found in the Mysteries are: the *Golden Legend,* the *Northern Passion,* the *Cursor Mundi* and the *Meditationes.*

[37] "Notes on the Home of Ludus Coventriae," in Swenson's *An Inquiry, etc.,* p. 82.

entrance there, calling forth ever renewed demand and production. Each ecclesiastical holiday was, if possible, to be solemnized by its special legend in English verse.[38]

It is possible, as ten Brink observes, that the *Golden Legend* may contain material of English origin. Ten Brink cites many similarities, and adds to this the fact that the *Golden Legend* was written at a period when the legend vogue was at its height in England.[39] Thus we can realize the extent and popularity of the legend among the people of England, and perhaps can form some idea of the ease with which legends of the Virgin, while traceable to apocrypha, could take root in the pious traditions of the English people, affecting even their art and their literature.[40] That is why the inclusion of apocryphal matter in the rôle of Mary appears in no way to denote a corrupted reverence either for Scripture itself or for the Virgin Mary. Such material does not alter her Christocentric rôle, any more than does the inclusion of genuine Scripture.

[38] Ten Brink, *op. cit.*, p. 266.

[39] *Ibid.*, p. 269.

[40] It is in view of this power of tradition among the medieval English that I think the statement of James anent the *Pseudo-Matthew Gospel* too doctrinaire: " The real importance of *Pseudo-Matthew* lies not so much in the stories which it preserves, as in the fact that it was the principal vehicle by which they were known to the Middle Ages and the principal source of inspiration to the artists and poets of the centuries from the twelfth to the fifteenth. It is upon this text that the many vernacular versions for the most part depend; and by this that the pictures of the Rejection of Joachim's offering, his meeting with Anne at the Golden Gate, the Presentation of the Virgin, the Repose in Egypt, and the few that we have of the Infancy Miracles, are inspired." (*The Apocryphal New Testament*, tr. by M. R. James, Oxford, 1924, p. 79.) Clearly it was not the text of this Gospel, but rather the traditions arising from it that affected the Middle Ages as James has described. We can hardly image such numerous texts, nor such widespread literacy of Latin among the common folk, particularly in England, to effect such popular knowledge of the apocrypha. In his article on " Apocrypha," G. J. Reid (*Catholic Encyclopedia*, I, 1913, p. 615) cites a work of Pope Benedict XIV, in which certain popular apocrypha then in circulation (seventeenth century) are declared " impure sources of tradition." This is, as Reid remarks, an echo of ancient ecclesiastical condemnations, which likewise were issued, doubtlessly, to prevent the rise of any traditions that might eventuate in heterodoxy.

A brief word remains anent the characteristics, so to speak, of each cycle in its handling of the Virgin's rôle. Coventry, to begin with, involves the Marian element more than any of the other cycles. Eighteen Coventry plays contain that element. This Marian prominence has led both Craig [41] and Chambers [42] to assign Lincoln as the home of the cycle, since that city was marked for its St. Anne cult, a cult closely allied to that of the Virgin Mary. Coventry, moreover, contains a distinct Virgin Group, as it is called, the theories concerning which I have already mentioned.[43] The Marian rôle in this cycle is very devotionally didactic; by that I mean we frequently meet with passages which seem to exhort the spectators to a greater devotion toward the Mother of God. For example, in the *Salutation and Conception,* we hear the angel Gabriel delivering a long and lyrical prayer of praise to her, in which he reviews many devotional aspects, addressing her as, lady highest of kindred, throne of the Trinity, queen of Heaven, lady of earth, empress of hell, succor to all sinful, mother of mercy, bond of Heaven and earth. This effusion ends amid angels singing, "Ave maria gratia plena Dominus tecum uirgo sesena." [44] Or again, in the *Trial of Joseph and Mary,* the tribute paid to the pure Virgin savors of a lesson on the dignity and immaculateness of the Mother of God. In the *Nativity, Shepherd* and *Magi* plays this doctrinal focus shifts almost entirely to the Christ Child, but returns to the Virgin in the *Purification,* diminishes in the Passion plays and resumes with its greatest vividness in the *Assumption.* However, in the York *Assumption* and *Coronation,* the devotional tendency of Coventry is surpassed. This didacticism, then, appears to be the great characteristic of Coventry's management of the Marian rôle. It exists so extensively throughout the cycle that the Marian element simply falls under its influence rather than receives it designedly. The cycle has also the most distributed *Planctus* ele-

[41] "Notes on the Home of Ludus Coventriae," in Swenson's *An Inquiry,* etc., p. 82 *passim.*
[42] *The Medieval State,* pp. 126-127.
[43] P. 27.
[44] In the text of the play this word was meant to appear as *serena,* as is evident by the correction which the scribe had begun to make. See Block, *Ludus Coventriae,* p. 108.

ment in the Passion plays, and here too the tendency to doctrinize is apparent, although the doctrine is mainly about the Mystery of the Redemption; still, Mary's divine maternity constantly figures wherever her *Planctus* is introduced.

The other three cycles have nothing very distinctive in their treatment of the Virgin. York, which contains fourteen plays involving her, depicts in general a gentler spouse of Mary than do the other cycles. She elicits a good deal more respect from Joseph, particularly in the *Flight into Egypt,* where the patriarch divides his time between comforting the Mother and carrying the Child. Towneley, as far as I am able to judge, has no noticeable individuality in its general dealing with the Virgin. As in York, but to a very smaller degree, Mary fares well at the hands of her spouse in the *Flight into Egypt,* but not until after Joseph has given full vent to his annoyance, including a confidential warning to all prospective husbands to beware of matrimony, for it is making him " all wan ". The one outstanding Marian feature in the Chester cycle is the absence of any remonstrance from Mary when she finds Christ with the Doctors.

But taking the cycles as a whole, we have seen that, however variant the functions of Mary's rôle, they preserve everywhere that Christocentric quality, or status, upon which no dramatic liberties are taken. I have devoted my study to unveiling that Christocentric status, not because anyone before me, as far as I know, has denied it, but chiefly because it appears to have been ignored or perhaps overlooked, among students of the English Medieval Drama. I think an adequate recognition of that status is important. It discloses something extraordinary: a leading dramatic figure that forbids any kind of exploitation for its own interest; a figure of prime theatrical interest, but one that is never isolated, never developed for its own sake. Mary is devoid of any selfish conflict. The dramatists have unanimously made it clear that if she is to be described in trouble, it is because she shares in the trouble of her Son. If she is lauded, it is because she walks in the shadow of the glory of that Son. She is the only figure of the cyclic stage (Christ excepted) thus consistently dramatized. Joseph's rôle, as we have seen, is wantonly treated, but Mary's preserves the

same underlying restraint and delicacy.   The same Christocentricity abides with it in every episode.

I do not wish to posit questions I cannot answer, at least in the
present work.   But it has occurred to me that the Christocentricity
of the Virgin's rôle, once recognized, may illuminate future research into the cyclic drama of Medieval England, or at least open
up new and fascinating byways of investigation.   It may throw
further light upon one or several much mooted questions, such as
the extent to which the liturgy influenced the Middle English
Drama, or what hand religious and ecclesiastics had in the composition of plays.   One thing, however, is certain: A definite and
uniform attitude of mind was brought to the Marian rôle in this
drama, and that attitude must have had its source in Catholic tradition.   Schelling, with rare insight, says:

> The sanctity of the momentous subject, the story of the Saviour, forbade
> inventive freedom to the writers and revisers of the cycles, who therefore
> expended their ingenuity on unimportant personages and details.[45]

Quite the same can be said of the Virgin's rôle, for, while there is
no dearth of inventive freedom, at least in the Marian dialogue,
a sense of momentous dignity, a very respectful and cautious attitude, prevents the various dramatists from exploiting Mary, and
drives them to expend their dramatic ingenuity upon lesser characters, such as St. Joseph.

[45] *English Drama*, New York, 1914, p. 23.

A BIBLIOGRAPHY OF WORKS REFERRED TO IN THIS STUDY

Adam, Le Mystère d', ed. by P. Studer, Manchester, 1918.

Anne, Life of, The Middle English Stanzaic Versions, ed. by R. E. Parker, EETS. OS. 174 (1928).

Apocryphal New Testament, The, ed. by M. R. James, Oxford, 1924.

Azarias, Brother, *Essays Miscellaneous*, Chicago, 1896.

Blessed Virgin, The, in the Fathers of the First Six Centuries, T. Livius, London, 1893.

Blickling Homilies, The, ed. by Morris, EETS. OS. 63 (1876).

Bonnell, John K., "The Source in Art of the So-Called Prophets Play in the Hegge Collection," in *PMLA*, 29 (1914).

Bridgett, T., *Our Lady's Dowry*, London, 1875.

Brown, C., *Religious Lyrics of the XIV Century*, Oxford, 1924.

Budge, Wallis, *Legends of Our Lady the Perpetual Virgin and Her Mother Hanna*, Boston, 1922.

Burgert, Edward, *The Dependence of Part I of Cynewulf's Christ upon the Antiphonary*, Washington, D. C., 1921.

Chambers, E. K., *Medieval Stage*, II, Oxford, 1903.

Chester Plays, ed. by H. Deimling and Matthews, EETS. ES. 62, 115 (1892, 1914).

Coffman, G., Review of Carghill's *Drama and Liturgy*, in *Speculum*, VI (1931), No. 4, 610-617.

Cornish Drama, Ancient, ed. by E. Norris, Oxford, I, 1859.

"Corpus Christi Play, The English, its Relation to the Middle English Religious Lyric," G. Taylor, in *Modern Philology*, V (1907).

Craig, Hardin, "Notes on the Home of Ludus Coventriae," in Swenson's *An Inquiry into the Composition and Structure of Ludus Coventriae*, Minneapolis, 1914.

Two Coventry Corpus Christi Plays, EETS. ES. 87 (1902).

Cursor Mundi, ed. by R. Morris. EETS. OS. 68 (1878).

Davidson, C., *Studies in the English Mystery Plays*, in *Transactions of Connecticut Academy of Sciences* 9, 1 (1892).

Fehr, B., *Die Hirtenbriefe Aelfrics* (Bibliothek der angels, prosa, Band IX), Hamburg, 1914.

Furnivall, F. J., ed. *Digby Plays*. EETS. ES. 70 (1896).

Ed. *Hoccleve's Minor Poems*, I. EETS. ES. 61 (1892).

Gayley, C. M., *Plays of Our Forefathers*, London, 1908.

Gerould, G., *Saints' Legends*, Boston, 1916.

Gesetze der Angelsachsen, F. Liebermann, Niemeyer, 1903-1916.

Gildersleeve, B. L., "Changes in Verse-Technic in the Sixteenth Century English Drama," in *American Journal of Philology*, No. 31 (1910).

119

Greg, W., *Bibliographical and Textual Problems of the English Miracle Cycles*, London, 1914.

Gueranger, Dom P., *The Liturgical Year*, Dublin, 1879.

Hackauf, E., *Die älteste mittelenglische Version der Assumptio Mariae*, Berlin, 1902.

Hemingway, E., *English Nativity Plays*, New York, 1909.

Hone, W., *Ancient Mysteries Described*, London, 1823.

Holweck, F. G., " The Immaculate Conception," in *Catholic Encyclopedia*, VII (1913).

" The Visitation of the B. V. M.," *Ibid.*, XV (1913).

" St. Anne," *Ibid.*, I (1913).

" Sorrows of the B. V. M.," *Ibid.*, XIV (1913).

Homilies, Old English, ed. by R. Morris, EETS. OS. 53 (1872).

Iconography, Early Christian, Smith, Princeton, 1922.

Kretzmann, P. E., *The Liturgical Element in the Earliest Forms of the Medieval Drama*, Minneapolis, 1916.

Kyng Horn, Floris and Blancheflur, etc., ed. G. H. McKnight. EETS. OS. 14 (1866).

Légende Dorée, La, ed. by Roze, III, Paris, 1902.

Life of Christ, The Stanzaic, ed. by F. Foster, EETS. OS. 166 (1926).

Ludus Coventriae, ed. by K. Block, EETS. ES. 120 (1917).

MacEvilly, *An Exposition of the Gospels (Matthew and Mark)*, New York, 1888.

Maldonatus, *A Commentary on the Holy Gospels*, tr. by Daviem, London, 1888.

Meals and Manners, Early English, ed. F. J. Furnivall, EETS. OS. 32 (1868).

Migne, J. P., *Patrologiae Latinae* 28, 60, 65, 98; *Patrologiae Graecae* 39, 32, 13.

Minor Poems of the Vernon Manuscript, ed. by F. J. Furnivall, EETS. OS. 117 (1901).

Miracle Plays, English, ed. Pollard, Oxford, 1909.

Mirk's Festial, ed. by Erbe, EETS. ES. 96 (1905).

Mirrour of the Blessed Lyf of Jesu Christ, N. Love, tr., London, 1908.

Mossman, *The Great Commentary of Cornelius à Lapide (St. Matthew, chapters I-IX)*, London, 1887.

Petit de Julleville, *Les Mystères*, II. Paris, 1880.

Les Comédiens en France au Moyen Âge. Paris, 1885.

Plainte de la Vierge, A. Linder. Upsala, 1898.

" Planctus Mariae, The English," G. Taylor, in *Modern Philology*, IV (1907).

Pourrat, P., *Christian Spirituality*, II, London, 1924.

Reany, W., *The Creation of the Human Soul*, New York, 1932.

Reid, G. J., " Apocrypha," in *Catholic Encyclopedia*, I (1913).

Sarum Missal, ed. by W. Legg, Oxford, 1916.

Schelling, F., *English Drama*, New York, 1914.

Schönbach, A., *Über die Marienklagen*, Leipsic, 1874.

Sepet, M., " Les Prophètes du Christ," in *Bibliothèque de l'École de Chartes,* XXVIII.

Skelton's Magnyfycence, ed. by Ramsy, EETS. ES. 98 (1906).

Souvay, " St. Joseph," in *Catholic Encyclopedia,* VIII (1913).

Swenson, E. L., *An Inquiry into the Composition and Structure of Ludus Coventriae,* Minneapolis, 1914.

Tanquerey, A., *The Spiritual Life,* Tournai, 1930.

Tanquerey, F., *Plaintes de la Vierge en Anglo-Français,* Paris, 1921.

Thien, H., *Über die Englischen Marienklagen,* Kiel Diss., 1906.

Ten Brink, *History of English Literature (Fourteenth Century to Surrey),* tr. by Brandl, New York, 1896.

Towneley Plays, The, ed. by G. England and A. W. Pollard, EETS. ES. 71 (1897).

Thurston, " The Hail Mary," in *The Catholic Encyclopedia,* VII (1913).

Travers, H., *Four Daughters of God,* Bryn Mawr Dissertation, 1907.

Vernet, F., *Medieval Spirituality,* London, 1930.

Vriend, J., *The Blessed Virgin Mary in the Medieval Drama of England,* Purmerend, Holland, 1928.

Ward, A. W., " The Drama to 1642," in *CHEL,* V (1910).

Wechssler, E., *Die Romanischen Marienklagen,* Halle, 1893.

Wells, *A Manual of the Writings in Middle English,* New Haven, 1916.

Woodward, G. R., *The Most Holy Mother of God in the Songs of the Eastern Church,* London, 1919.

York and Towneley Cycles, the Original Identity of, M. Lyle, University of Minnesota Dissertation, 1919.

York Mystery Plays, ed. by L. T. Smith, Oxford, 1885.

Young, K., " Observations on the Origin of the Medieval Passion Play," in *PMLA,* XXV (1910).